Connecticut Ghosts

Spirits in the State of Steady Habits

Elaine M. Kuzmeskus, M.S.

4880 Lower Valley Road, Atglen, PA 19310 USA

Published by Schiffer Publishing Ltd.
4880 Lower Valley Road
Atglen, PA 19310
Phone: (610) 593-1777; Fax: (610) 593-2002
E-mail: Info@schifferbooks.com

For the largest selection of fine reference books on this and related subjects, please
visit our web site at **www.schifferbooks.com**
We are always looking for people to write books on new and related subjects. If you
have an idea for a book please contact us at the above address.

This book may be purchased from the publisher.
Include $3.95 for shipping.
Please try your bookstore first.
You may write for a free catalog.

In Europe, Schiffer books are distributed by
Bushwood Books
6 Marksbury Ave.
Kew Gardens
Surrey TW9 4JF England
Phone: 44 (0) 20 8392-8585; Fax: 44 (0) 20 8392-9876
E-mail: info@bushwoodbooks.co.uk
Free postage in the U.K., Europe; air mail at cost.

Copyright © 2006 by Elaine M. Kuzmeskus
Library of Congress Control Number: 2005930480

Designed by Natalie Baer
Type set in University Roman Bd BT/Dutch801 Rm BT

ISBN: 0-7643-2361-X
Printed in China

Dedication

This book is lovingly dedicated to my grandparents: Harry and Katherine Brickett. Grandpa taught me to search for the truth, while Nana advised: "There is no need to be afraid of the people who have died – it's the ones who are alive that you have to watch out for."

Acknowledgments

I would like to thank my friend and editor, Susan Roberts, for her expert editing and encouragement throughout this project. This our third project together and I cannot imagine doing a book without her. Next, I would like to thank, Tina Skinner, Schiffer Publishers, for suggesting the book and her good-natured support.

My husband, Ronald Kuzmeskus, who fearlessly walked the woods of Dudleytown, mines of Old New-Gate Prison, and many an old mansion in search of ghosts, was a huge help. I also wish to thank Marianne Alibozak, who kindly volunteered to take photographs, as well as student photographer, Richard Doak Jr., and parapsychology student, Maureen Forrester for their assistance.

Finally, I would like to acknowledge the many generous staff members of Connecticut's museums and historical sites. Hill-Stead Museum Curator, Cynthia Cormier, and Curatorial Assistant, Melanie Anderson Bourbeau, gave unstintingly of their time and knowledge; as did the staffs at the Connecticut State Library, the Harriet Beecher Stowe Center, and Mark Twain House and Museum, and Old New-Gate Prison.

Contents

Introduction

A Medium's Perspective

Even though I have been a Spiritualist medium for thirty years, I had never thought of writing a book on ghosts, quite simply because they are so much a part of my everyday life. I wake up to spirit messages such as "Don't forget to mail Judy's gift." or "That chapter needs tweaking." The spirits then follow me through my daily work as a medium. Even as I turn in for the night, I see a cluster of lights overhead. Often when I attend a play the Bushnell, I see ghosts and angelic beings assisting the performance. In fact, the first things I notice when visiting a hospital, church or library are the spirits who cohabitate. People would be surprised to see the many spirit doctors who still practice medicine!

Ghosts come in especially strong when visiting historic homes, such as the Mark Twain or Harriet Beecher Stowe home. These ghost love attention and, if tourists are not noticing them enough, a breeze may stir, a light flicker, or a cat may cross a path. All these are signs that something supernatural is afoot.

At the Mark Twain home, the spirits of three Victorian ladies were sitting on the round velvet sofa in the spacious entryway waiting to greet visitors. One resembled Susie Clemens, Mark Twain's daughter, who died in the house at twenty-four. The other, an older woman and more plainly attired, resembled Mrs. Twain's maid, and the third—a middle-aged lady smartly dressed in black with a black Victorian bonnet that looked like Oliva's,

Mark Twain's wife. They seemed to know I was ghost hunting and were acting as a welcome committee from the other side.

When spirits are around, they often send calling cards. For example, as I was taking picture around the Harriet Beecher Stowe home, which is just a stone's throw from the Twain mansion, two bright blue butterflies came out of nowhere and continued to cross my path. Butterflies are a symbol of immortality, quite appropriate as both Harriet Beecher Stowe and her husband, Captain Stowe, believed in Spiritualism. As I tuned into the energy of the house, they seemed happy—almost joyful—to have visitors. Harriet Beecher Stowe whose book, *Uncle Tom's Cabin*, championed abolition, would have been delighted to tell the world, "There is no death and there are no dead."

Not only were the Stowes devout believers, but so was the Cheney family in Manchester. When I visited the Cheney Homestead, I could not help but notice the large mahogany table that dominated the second floor family room. As if she were reading my mind, Arlene, the housekeeper, spoke up: "The Cheneys used to hold séances in this room." Next, I noticed a portrait of Kate Fox, the woman who started the Spiritualist movement in the United States, was proudly displayed. Her magnetic brown eyes seemed to follow me wherever I went in the room. On closer examination, I saw the handsome image of the brunette young woman was painted by Seth Cheney. My husband, Ron, also felt the intense vibration of the room, and we both saw several orbs of light near the painting and in back of the "séance" table. "I would love to get picture of this room," I thought. Alas, no picture taking was permitted.

Theodate Pope, another Connecticut citizen, also had a lot of psychic activity in her home — Hill-Stead House. The formal parlor filled with antique furniture upholstered in rose also had a round table positioned in the center of the room.

Was it also used for séances? The tour guide had no idea. Even more energy was present in the library. Spirit light started flashing immediately when I entered the room, directing me to a corner of the library. As I browsed the shelves, I noticed they were filled with books on parapsychology. Besides being a premier architect, who designed the Avon Old Farm School for Boys, Theodate Pope was a champion of parapsychology research. "What stories these walls could tell if only they could talk," I thought. Theodate Pope, I am sure, would gladly have invited a visitor into her library to share her passion for parapsychology. One of her dreams was to establish a parapsychology research facility in Connecticut, similar to the British Society for Psychical Research in London.

Other places were less welcoming though. The spirits trapped in the coppers mines of New-Gate Prison were still hard at work, as shown by the spirit orbs present in the mines. Furthermore, Dudleytown was downright unfriendly. The energy seemed to extend about a mile around. It was not until we drove past the banks of the Housatonic River, where American Indians used to fish, that I felt calm. No wonder it is called the "Most Haunted Town in the United States."

There were many locations that held a special memory for the families that used to live there. When I visited the Shaw Mansion in New London, a whole group — mothers, fathers, and small children — greeted me on the second floor landing where the Shaw family was known to socialize two hundred years ago. Their eager orbs jumped out from the picture taken on the second floor sitting area.

Other spirits were still guarding their turf. I felt the presence of Adelma Simmons, for example, as I walked through the gardens of Carpilands. She shook her spirit head at the sight of the many herb plots in need of weeding. Mrs. Simmons' energy was especially strong by one of the many statues of Saint Frances that guarded the grounds, as well as behind the counter in her herb shop.

While Caprilands seems to have limited funds, Gillette Castle just received a two million dollar facelift. That would have pleased its owner, Victorian actor William Gillette. His spirit still shines in his retirement castle, complete with a small railroad and a boat. When I entered the third floor library and art gallery, I asked the security guard about all the cat pictures. "Apparently he was quite a character," she said. "He really loved cats, had about nine of them — even gave parties for his cats on his boat, the *Aunt Polly*."

Of course, not all homes are happy, some are dysfunctional. Such was the case of the couple who lived in what is now the Red Brook in Mystic. The husband, it seems, had a mistress whom he later married after his first wife died following a long battle with cancer. However, the spirit of the first wife was not pleased when the second wife had a birthday party at their old home, which had now become the Red Brook Inn. She got her spooky revenge when the birthday cake literally exploded as her former mate sliced the first piece of carrot cake!

I had many chuckles as I researched this book. Sometimes people even interviewed me when I introduced myself as a medium who was researching a book on ghosts in Connecticut. The first question I was asked was, "How did you become a medium?" My reply, " I was born with the gift of clairvoyance." However, as with other natural clairvoyants, such as Andrew Jackson Davis, Edgar Cayce, and Eileen Garret, the gift left me feeling out of sync with the rest of the world. We live in a society that views individuals seeing things as psychotic. Until I read Edgar Cayce's biography, *The Sleeping Prophet,* by Jess Stearn, I was very quiet about my clairvoyance. Just knowing there was another person, Edgar Cayce, who also talked to ghosts was a tremendous relief.

Another question, I was often asked was, "Aren't you afraid of ghosts?" "No, not really," is my reply. After all, I have been in touch with spirits all my life. Ever since I can recall, I have been able to close my eyes and see a guide present — at first it was a slightly built, bare-chested Hindu clothed in a white muslin dhoti and matching turban. Later, it was a handsome Egyptian master wearing a striped headdress with a cobra rising from the middle of his forehead — a spot I would later call the third eye. Just looking into my guide's magnetic brown eyes would make my head swirl, so intense was the master's gaze. Later, as I began to do readings for others, an ancient Chinese doctor came in to assist. Clairvoyantly, I could see the blacked robed physician with a black pillbox hat examining the unsuspecting sitter's pulse. While the Hindu, Egyptian, and Chinese masters did not give their names, other guides did — notably Dr. Lang. For several months, I heard the name "Dr Lang" pop up clairaudiently as I did readings for clients. When I enquired of the spirit, "Who are you?" Dr Lang explained patiently that he, too, had been inter-ested in parapsychology. After some research, I found that a Dr. Andrew Lang had indeed been an early turn of the twentieth century researcher.

With so many guides by my side, I felt very protected as I did the research for this book. In fact, I feel protected most of the time. As my Irish grandmother told me years ago, "There is no need to be afraid of the people who have died – it's the ones who are alive that you need to watch!" I hope when you finish reading *Connecticut Ghosts* you will feel the same way. Most ghosts are not out to hurt you, and the few mischievous ones are only trying to get our attention. In fact, Connecticut's ghosts were, for the most part, quite hospitable.

Chapter One

Witchcraft in Colonial Connecticut

Connecticut, home to insurance giants — Travelers, Aetna, Cigna, and the Hartford, is known as a state of steady habits. The colony, after all, was formed by the practical Dutch settlers from Manhattan Island and the sober Puritans from Massachusetts. The Dutch, who arrived first, built a fort in Hartford. In 1633, the English sailed in and built their trading post in Windsor — much to the chagrin of Dutch. A few years later, in July 1635, the English formed a settlement in Wethersfield. The next year, Rev. Thomas Hooker moved his congregation from Cambridge to the Connecticut colony, founding the town of Hartford. Many who settled in Connecticut remained true to their Puritan and Dutch ancestors — willing to work hard and save to insure a secure future. Solid citizens who did not allow idle chatter or superstition to disrupt a day's work populated Hartford, Wethersfield, and Windsor. Their efforts paid off, creating the vast fortunes in tobacco, manufacturing, banking, and insurance.

The state became known for its steady habits – its capital, Hartford, the insurance center of North America. Few would associate Connecticut with the paranormal. When the word witch is spoken, images of Salem, Massachusetts, come to mind. No one would even think of Windsor, Connecticut. Yet that is where the first woman was put to death for witchcraft in the New World. Alis Young was executed in Windsor, Connecticut – not Salem .In fact, more witches were put to death in Connecticut then the

Salem, Massachusetts. Forty-five individuals were put to death for the crime of witchcraft in Connecticut from 1647 to 1887; yet, few people connect Connecticut with witch-hunts.

Our frugal ancestors also had a dark side — the persecution of anyone involved with the occult arts, collectively known as witchcraft. The majority of those who settled the Connecticut colonies emigrated from Essex, England — the witchcraft capital of England. They brought with them not only their steady habits but also a strong belief in witchcraft. The early settlers took a dim view on witches, whom they considered to be consorting with the devil. In 1642 the Connecticut colony made witchcraft a felony crime on par with murder, rape, and treason. While some accused of witchcraft may have been malevolent citizens or schizophrenic souls, many were intuitive folk.

However, psychic arts were not in vogue in the colonies. In fact, of all the crimes in Connecticut, witchcraft was considered diabolical. The colonists, who looked to the Bible for guidance, took seriously the laws of Moses written in Exodus II, verse 18: "If any man or woman be a witch, hath or consulteth with a familiar spirit, they shall be put to death." In the colony of Connecticut, practicing witchcraft was punishable by a death sentence.

During the first century of the colony's existence, over thirty witches were put to death. Most lived in the Hartford area, but there were also some from Fairfield, New Haven, Saybrook, and Wallingford. Alis Young of Windsor was the first victim in 1647. Little is known about her, save the fact that she was the wife of John Young and was hanged on May 26, 1647, according to Windsor town clerk Mathew Grant. What exactly did she do? Did she bewitch others with spells or consult with unfamiliar spirits? Many at the time believed that a witch could appear in the form of an animal, thus causing accidents and damage to property — or even death to animals or humans. Had someone accused her of taking the form of a black cat or a red fox and causing mischief? Another possibility was the mark of the devil. Did she have any deformity or unusual making on her body that caused suspicion? Because of the lack of detailed records, it would seem that Alis Young was a woman of little consequence. She may well have just been a simple woman without the guile or social influence needed for a defense against the accusation of the crime of witchcraft rather than the servant of the devil.

Over the next seventeen years, fourteen more people came under suspicion. In 1648, Mary Johnson from Wethersfield confessed to Rev. Cotton Mather that "the devil was wont to do her many services," admitting freely to licentiousness and the murder of a child. One wonders why Mary Johnson confessed. Was it to protect others or had the fear of God been put into her by her accusers? Even though she repented, she was hanged on Gallow's Hill, just north of Trinity College.

Many witches, it seems, were tried on hearsay, gossip, or forced confessions. Such may have been the case of a Wethersfield carpenter, John Carrington, and his wife, Joanne, in 1651. Carrington already had an unsavory reputation from raiding guns with the Indians. When they were accused of "ffamilarity with Sathan the great enemye of God and mankinde," the charge stuck. Sadly, both Carringtons were found guilty and hung for their crime.

A Lydia Gilbert of Windsor was then accused of employing witchcraft in the death of Henry Stiles, some three years earlier. His death had been ruled an accidental homicide when a gun owned by a neighbor accidentally discharged. However, according to the court, Lydia Gilbert had used her evils powers to cause the gun to go off. Why did it take three years for the charge to be made?

Next, Goody (short for goodwife or Mrs.) Bassett and Goody Knapp, both respectable women, were found guilty of witchcraft.

To their credit, both died refusing to give the names of others supposedly involved with witchcraft. Goody Knapp's corpse was even examined for witch's teats (extra nipples and breasts) but none were found. The fact that no witch's marks were found did little to clear her name.

The largest of the witch hunts in the mid-1600s occurred in Hartford, Connecticut. Eight people were accused of the heinous crime of witchcraft, and three of the eight, including Nathaniel and Rebecca Greensmith, were put to death. A fourth, Mary Barnes, may also have been killed. The hysteria began with Ann Cole, a wealthy woman who was a religious fanatic. She became ill with what she termed "diabolical possession." When she went into fits, strange voices would speak through her — similar to what is called multiple personality disorder. Since Ann Cole claimed she had no recollections of these voices, it is likely she was a in trance state. Cole even spoke in Dutch, a language she was not familiar with, while in a trance.

Ann Cole's voices accused Nathaniel and Rebecca Greensmith of witchcraft. She also accused Elizabeth Seagar, who was later found guilty and released after a year in jail. The Greensmiths were not as fortunate. They were put to the water test in which the right thumb was tied to the left toe and left thumb to the right toe. Somehow tied in this cruel fashion, each managed to stay afloat. The townspeople used this as evidence they had made a pack with the devil, for otherwise they would have drown. While Nathaniel stuck to his story of innocence, Rebecca broke down and confessed her guilt, claiming lewd acts, chief among which was admission that "the devil had frequent carnal knowledge of her body." Both Greensmiths were found guilty and executed in 1661.

Only after all the witches either fled or were put to death did Ann Cole regain her health. Later, she benefited from the Greensmiths' deaths when she married Andrew Benton, a widower who bought the property the couple was forced to give up. Not unlike Salem, much of the testimony against the witches in Connecticut came from hysterical children. For example, dying eight-year-old Elizabeth Kelly made the accusation, "Goody Ayres torments me, she pricks me with pins, she will kill me" The youngster continued to suffer in her bed through the next day. Her last words were, "Goodwife Ayres chokes me." When his daughter died, John Kelly had Goody Ayres and her husband, William, who had a reputation as a thief, arrested for witchcraft. The Ayres wisely fled for their lives.

An ulterior motives may also have figured in the case of Elizabeth Garlick, a woman accused of witchcraft in East Hampton. Her neighbor, Sarah Howell, who herself was showing signs of witchcraft practice, accused Garlick of torturing and pricking her body with pins. Thus Howell explained her own uncontrollable twitching. She further claimed to see a black form with a double tongue appear over her bed, threatening her life. Was Sarah Howell hallucinating or giving fake testimony to save her own life?

Even as late as 1753, the hysteria over witches continued in the state. A maiden lady, forty-four year old Juliana Fox, was convicted that year for having two marks on a left shoulder exposed when she was knocked down by hunting dogs belonging to Julius Perry. Her version of the story was Mr. Perry had set his dogs on her when she fought off his attempts to rape her. The crowd in the courtroom did not believe her and shouted, "Burn the witch!"

Were these witchcraft accusations made out of spite, envy, greed, hysteria of children, or madness? Some scientists believe the hallucinations may have been brought on by a fungus ergot found in rye. Other biological explanations would include chronic chorea associated with dementia, schizophrenia, or Alzheimer's disease. How many "witches" were victims of ergot or chorea, schizophrenia or Alzheimer's? Who knows for sure? One thing is certain, the good people of colonial Connecticut took witchcraft very seriously. Few would even entertain the possibility that many of those condemned to death for communicating with familiar spirits may well have been Connecticut's first mediums.

Chapter Two
Séances Around Victorian Hartford

Séances were the rage in Victorian America and Connecticut was no exception. Prestigious Connecticut families — the Beechers of Hartford and the Cheneys of South Manchester — played host to Katherine Fox, the medium who began the Spiritualist movement. In 1847 she and her sister heard rapping in their Hydesville, New York, cottage. Soon they began to communicate with the spirit of an itinerant peddler who claimed he had been murdered and his body buried beneath their dirt cellar. From these modest beginnings, the two sisters, Katherine and Margaret Fox, began to give public demonstrations of their remarkable mediumship. Horace Greeley was so impressed that he enthusiastically endorsed the Fox sisters' mediumistic gifts in the *New York Tribune*.

Connecticut was also host to the most famous physical medium of the day, Daniel Douglas Home (1831-1886), who hailed from New London. Born in Scotland to a father who was a carpenter by trade and a mother who was clairvoyant, the family relocated to the United States, when Home was nine. At nineteen, he experienced his first levitation. Home also had the ability to stretch his body an additional two inches. He toured the world demonstrating his outstanding physical mediumship. Many, including Elizabeth Barrett Browning, were fascinated by his mediumship. Her husband, Poet Robert Browning, was less than enchanted, referring to Home was "Mr. Sludge, the Medium." Sir

William Crookes, the scientist who tested Home in the laboratory, was impressed. Dr. Crookes validated Home's mediumship, much to the dismay of Home's critics.

D. D. Home was a popular guest of the silk manufacturing family founded by Timothy Cheney. He visited the Cheneys several times at their homes in Manchester. In August of 1852, while at the home of Ward Cheney, he moved beyond mediumship and levitated. Fortunately, a local journalist, F.L. Burr, was present to give this account:

> Suddenly, without any expectation of the part of the company, Home was taken up into the air. I had hold of his hand at the time and I felt his feet — they were lifted a foot from the floor.

It wasn't long before a surprised Home reached the ceiling. A few years later, Homes amazed Lord Adler and his London guests by levitating out one third-story window and into the next. Scientists witnessed bells, a guitar, and an accordion being played by invisible hands at a distance from the medium.[1]

Talented mediums such as D.D. Home caught the attention of the American public and journalists such as Horace Greeley (1811-1872). Impressed by the quality of mediumship, Greeley opened columns in his newspaper for those who wished to bring through messages from spirits.

Other Americans prominent in the Spiritualist movement included Professor J.S. Loveland, who wrote the first American book on Spiritualism, *Esoteric Truths of Spiritualism*; James Peebles (1822-1922), a medical doctor and a Universalist minister wrote *What is Spiritualism?* and *Seers Through the Ages*; and later, Emma Hardings Britten founded the Spiritualist publication, *Two Worlds*.

Britten's teacher, Ada Foye, was the target of Mark Twain's humor. After seeing her séance in San Francisco, Twain wrote a short story, "Among the Spiritualists." According to Twain's account, "There was an audience of about 400 ladies and gentlemen present, and plenty of newspaper people — neuters. I saw a good-looking, earnest-faced, pale-red-haired, neatly dressed, young woman standing on a little stage behind a small deal table with slender legs and no drawers — the table, understand me; I am writing in a hurry, but I do not desire to confound my description of the table with my description of the lady. The lady was Mrs. Foye." Twain goes on to give a comical description of Ada Foye's efforts to contact two individuals at his request, the first a gambler, Gus (about whom Twain wrote, "It was no use trying to catch a departed gambler") and the second a gentleman with the surname of "Smith." Twain reported, "I got hold of the right Smith at last — the particular Smith I was after — my dear, lost, lamented friend — and learned that he died a violent death. I feared as much. He said his wife talked him to death. Poor wretch!"

While Mark Twain was not partial to mediums, he had a lifelong interest in the paranormal. As a young man he foresaw his brother, Henry Clemens', untimely death. In a vivid dream he saw the handsome twenty-year-old laid out in a metal coffin supported on two chairs with a vase containing a red flower placed next him. The vivid dream seemed real to Samuel Clemens, who was working on a riverboat with his brother at the time. Later, he got into a scrape with a member of the crew and left the boat at before its St. Louis destination – not wishing to cause further friction. That decision may have saved Twain's life. Later, the riverboat blew up. Henry Clemens, who was working in the boiler room at the time, was burned beyond recovery. Touched by the sight of Henry's youthful face, the ladies took up a collection of sixty dollar and purchased a metallic casket for the handsome young man. When Twain entered the room where the bodies were kept, he saw his brother just as he had been in the dream, except for the red flower. A few minutes later, an elderly lady brought in a pitcher of white flowers with one red rose in the center.[2]

Mark Twain had another psychic experience after his daughter Jean was found dead in a bathtub. When he entered the bathroom after her death he felt a cool breeze and thought, "Jean is this you trying to let me know you found the others" – referring to her baby brother Langdon, her sister Susie, and mother Olivia, who died before Jean.[3]

Mark Twain not only foresaw his brother's death in a dream, but received material in dreams. He also met dead relatives and friends in dreams. In his *Notebook* he described conversations with "the living and dead, rational and irrational." Apparently he was willing to investigate the idea of survival past death, for Mark Twain was also a member of the Society for Psychic Research, formed in 1882 to study spirit survival and mediumship. Researchers such Frederick W. H. Myers, Henry Sedgwick, Frank Podmore, Edward Gurney, and Richard Hodgson compiled an impressive amount of positive evidence and established a foundation for further scientific enquiry.[4]

Twain and his family lived in a tightly knit community on the outskirts of Hartford known as Nook Farm. Among the Nook Farm residents was Harriet Beecher Stowe, author of *Uncle Tom's Cabin*. When Harriet Beecher Stowe's half sister, Isabella Beecher Hooker, invited Twain to dinner, the elderly gentleman accepted the invitation. When he learned Isabella Beecher Hooker was having a medium for an after dinner séance, he made fun of the idea. Unfortunately, Mrs. Hooker heard of his jest and withdrew the invitation in a letter, enclosing a pamphlet on Spiritualism, which Twain promptly tore up![5]

Isabella Beecher Hooker took Spiritualism very seriously. She may well have been introduced to séances through her sister, Harriet Beecher Stowe. Even though her half sister often publically said she did approve of mediumship — believing that her noble ancestors would not stoop to coming through a medium, she still indulged privately in séances in her home for thirty years. Any interest Isabella Beecher Hooker had early in life was certainly fanned by her friendship with the Spiritualist leader Victoria Woodhull.

The friendship between the Hartford aristocrat, Isabella Hooker, and the medium from the lower-classes would have caused a stir in class-conscious Victorian Hartford. Woodhull's father, Buck Chaflin, was a petty thief and her mother was given to dabbing in mediumship. She and her sister, Tennessee, were "liberated women" long before woman even had the right to vote. In 1872, she was the first woman to run for President of the United States, nominated by the Equal Rights Party. Victoria Woodhull was also national president of the national Spiritualist association. She felt it was her divine duty to run for the highest office of the land. Woodhull also had her own funds to finance a campaign as she owned a stock brokerage firm, Woodhall and Chaflin, and was publisher of the New York journal, *Woodhull and Chaflin Weekly*. Her platform was a progressive one advocating an eight-hour workday, graduated income tax, and social welfare, as well as a woman's right to choose her romantic mate.

The public was offended by the latter view and called her everything from a witch to a prostitute. Dubbed "Mrs. Satan" when she spoke in Hartford, both she and Isabella Beecher Hooker were satirized in a *Hartford Courant* cartoon. Things went from bad to worse when Mrs. Woodhull was accused of taking on married lovers. At first, she did the prudent thing; she simply ignored the rumors that she believed were started by Catherine and Harriet Beecher Stowe. Then, stung with hurt, she fought back. She and her husband, Colonel Youngblood, wrote to Rev. Henry Ward Beecher, asking him to intercede on her behalf. Rev. Beecher ignored their request for help.

What happened next was the talk of Hartford. Woodhull publicly denounced Henry Ward Beecher for his own adultery, accusing the Rev Beecher of having an affair with a member of his congregation, one Libby Tilton, unhappy wife of Theodore Tilton, who was known to go into tirades over Libby's spending and even locked his wife in her room. When her marriage was at its lowest point, Libby sought solace with her minister, Rev Henry Ward Beecher, whose own wife was often mistaken for his mother. Libby, not in the least discreet, wrote to her husband about Rev Beecher, "Now I think I have lived a richer, happier life since I have known him. And have you not loved me more ardently since you saw another high nature appreciate me." When Theodore Tilton returned home, he had angry words with his wife, who tearfully confessed that she had had an "improper relation" with Rev. Beecher.[6] In the end, Tilton forgave his errant wife.

The whole matter would have rested there, except for Victoria Woodhull's accusation of Rev. Beecher's adultery. The Beechers, with the exception of Isabella, sided with their brother. As might be expected, all parties — the Rev. Henry Beecher, Libby Tilton, and her husband Theodore Tilton — denied everything. They said Victoria Woodhull was lying. The Beecher family even enlisted the help of the United States Marshals and the YMCA. As a result, the first female presidential candidate was arrested under the Comstock Act for sending "obscene" literature though the mail and spent election day in jail! After the scandal cooled off, Theodore Tilton had a change of heart. In 1875, he sued Henry Ward Beecher for alienation of his wife's affection. While it would appear Vicotroia Woodhull was right in the allegation of adultery, others simply shrugged Theodore Tilton off as another mean-spirited individual trying to bring down the good Reverend

Beecher.

As for Isabella Beecher Hooker, she continued her association with Victoria Woodhull, taking a tour of Europe in 1876 with her. In her Paris hotel, Isabella had a vision in which her mother, Harriet Porter Beecher, appeared in spirit to advise her. Isabella became a medium – however, a fanatical one. She would irritate family members with unwanted warnings from spirits concerning matters such as a future burglary. Since many of the events she foretold did not take place, family members (especially her daughter Katherine) were understandably irritated with Isabella. Conservative family members found her an embarrassment.

Her husband, John Hooker, also was concerned. While he believed in Spiritualism, he felt that his wife went too far, descending into "monomania" or "obsession" with the topic. Eventually, Isabella's daughter Katherine broke with her mother because of Isabella's obsession with communicating with the spirit world, which Isabella could now do on her own without the aid of a medium. While her daughter shut Isabella out, her granddaughter, Katherine Seymour Day, shared her spiritual leanings. The young girl would spend hours with her grandmother discussing the topic and watching as her grandmother communicated with the other side. When Isabella Hooker died in 1907 the controversy did not die as *The Hartford Courant* ran the headline," Mrs. Hooker Talks With Spirits"[7]

Isabella Beecher Hooker may have been ridiculed for talking with the spirits, but she was only one of many Victorians searching for answers from the world of spirits. In 1882 the Society for Psychical Research was formed to study spirit survival and mediumship and researchers such as Frederick W. H. Myers, Henry Sedgwick, Frank Podmore, Edward Gurney, and Richard Hodgson complied an impressive amount of positive evidence and established a foundation for further scientific enquiry.

By the turn of the century investigation into mediumship was in full swing in Boston, following Harvard professor William James's publication of *Varieties of Religious Experience* in 1902. James also studied a well-known medium of the day, Leonora Piper, for a period of twenty years. Piper became a medium in 1883 when she visited another medium known to give health readings. Before Leonora Piper knew it, she herself was in trance channeling a girl, Chlorine. By the time William James met her in 1885, Piper was an accomplished medium.[8] In fact, James was such a staunch believer of Piper's mediumship, that he presented a 100-page account of spirit communication in the *Proceedings of the American for Psychical Research* in 1909. James surprised the scientific community by including a verbatim record of his conversation with the spirit of the late Richard Hodgson in the journal.[9]

Theodate Pope Riddle knew William James and his brother, the author Henry James, well and had both brothers as houseguests at Hill-Stead, her Farmington, Connecticut, residence. Pope was so intrigued by the idea of spirit survival that she readily agreed to fund part of James's psychical research at Harvard, which focused on Leonora Piper's mediumship. In many ways, Theodate Pope Riddle was a woman who was a century ahead of her time. In an era where education was targeted for young gentlemen, while gentlewomen were discouraged from professional life, Theodate Pope made a name for herself in a man's field — architecture. One of her finest achievements was Avon Old Farms School in Avon, Connecticut. She surprised many when she married at forty-nine. She also had the courage to take in foster children later in life. Unfortunately, her first foster son, Gordon, died at age four. Even though saddened by Gordon's death, Theodate Pope Riddle did not give up on motherhood and took in two more boys on whom she doted.

She also had another passion — parapsychology. Not only did she read voraciously on the subject, as evidenced by the shelves at

Hill-Stead House, but she funded research into parapsychology both in Boston and New York. She even had session with Mrs. Piper. According to her biography, *Dearest of Geniuses,* Pope's interest in parapsychology was not just a passing fancy. She was known to have séances in Hill-Stead House. Often she would travel to New York to attend meetings at the American Society for Psychical Research. She was planning to establish a society in Connecticut. In fact, the year before she married, she and her maid were on a mission to visit the British Society for Psychical Research on the ill-fated ship *Lusitania.* As fate would have it, she survived the ship's sinking — but just barely.

While Theodate Pope Riddle did not accomplish her desire to establish a society for psychical research in the Hartford area, her ardent interest in spirit communication can be seen in the titles of the many books housed in the library of the home she designed in Farmington, Hill-Stead. She even invited mediums in to give séances. Unfortunately, few records remain of the séances, but her remarkable spirit is very evident at Hill-Stead — which she left as a museum. Connecticut visitors who tour the elegant estate may be impressed by the French Impressionist paintings and stately décor of the mansion, but few realize how very much Theodate Pope Riddle would have liked to introduce psychical research to Connecticut as well as fine architecture.

THE BEECHER FAMILY

Photograph of the Lyman Beecher Family (circa 1860). *Archives Harriet Beecher Stowe Center.*

Opposite page:
Photograph of Isabella Beecher
Hooker, Alice Hooker Day, and
Katherine Seymour Day. *Archives
Harriet Beecher Stowe Center.*

Opposite page: Mark Twain with his daughter Susie (circa 1860). *Archives: Mark Twain House, Hartford, CT.*

"A Garden is a place of healing to the soul ..." Harriet Beecher-Stowe House, Hartford, Connecticut. *Photographer: Elaine Kuzmeskus.*

Chapter Three

Ghost Hunting

Ghosts are everywhere and they especially enjoy contacting their loved ones on this side of life. Recently, a client, "Laura," told me this amazing story of spirit assistance. Laura had come to me many times to contact her deceased husband, "Ernie." A widow in her late thirties, Laura was left as the sole support of the couple's only child — a son, "Adam." Laura wanted to send her thirteen year old to one of Connecticut's best prep schools. With only a mother's pride, she enrolled Adam for the fall semester. Somehow, she "knew" that she would find a way to borrow the money for tuition. However, when her local bank turned her down, she was disheartened. Shortly thereafter, Laura's boss sent her on an assignment from her Hartford office across the state to a Norwalk facility. Unfamiliar with the roads, Laura ended up in Danbury where she stopped at a fast food restaurant for a Coke and directions. When she casually opened the small card attached to the drink, she received the surprise of her life. She had won the grand prize — one million dollars!

When Laura arrived for her annual reading, she shared the amazing story with me, adding "I am positive that Ernie is behind this." Sure enough, during the course of the reading, the spirit of her deceased husband came through to explain how he had used telepathy to guide his wife to the fast food restaurant. Telepathy or a "gut feeling" is by far the most common form of communication between the ghosts and the living. However, many people, unlike Laura, simply ignore telepathic thought, often to their disadvantage.

How do mediums communicate with these spirits? Several methods are employed — telepathy, clairaudience and clairvoyance, and trance being the most common. Telepathy is mind-to-mind communication in which the medium receives mental impressions from a spirit. It is also known as "clairscience" — French for clear feeling.

Another attribute of mediumship is clairaudience, French for clear hearing. When a medium literally hears a spirit speaking, he or she can accurately relay details such as names and dates. The late Rev. Arthur Ford was known for this gift. At a time when most mediums provided only first names of the so-called dead, Ford gave first and last names of the deceased with equal ease. For example, in a reading for Rev. Sun Myung Moon, on March 18, 1965, his guide Fletcher brought through the names of "Colonel Kousik," a deceased Korean statesman, and " Kim Koo," a martyred patriot from Korea.

The third quality of mediumship is clairvoyance — French for clear seeing. A clairvoyant is able to see spirits, often in fine detail. Many mediums such as Sylvia Browne and George Anderson are clairvoyants. For example, Sylvia Browne uses clairvoyance in her psychic detective work and ghost hunting. Early in her career, she was hired to investigate a haunted house in California for the TV program, "Sightings." Clairvoyantly, Ms. Browne was able to contact the unhappy spirit of a young woman who had lived in the bungalow back in the 1920s. As the medium quickly walked around the grounds of the property, she sensed sadness. Apparently the home belonged to the young woman with a gangster boyfriend. Left alone for long periods, the depressed woman just gave up and walked into the ocean. With Sylvia Browne's assistance, the unhappy spirit was able to go to the light, leaving a quieter house for the new owners.

The next level of mediumship is deep trance channeling. Edgar Cayce was well known for his ability to leave his body and conduct a reading in a deep trance state. While Cayce was known more for his medical clairvoyance, other trance mediums — notably Arthur Ford, Eileen Garrett, and Helen Duncan — focused on communicating with spirits. Duncan had the extraordinary ability to materialize spirits by gathering ectoplasm while sitting in a cabinet. The spirit then is molded from the vaporous substance. In the 1930s, many flocked to her cabinet séances held in Spiritualist churches in England. During World War II, Helen Duncan materialized the full form of a sailor with name of H.M.S. *Barham* embroidered on his cap. His message to his mother was poignant, but the British government, who wished to keep the ship's sinking a secret, were less than impressed. In fact, they had Duncan arrested as a spy. Fortunately, due to ardent supporters such as Chief Air Marshall Lord Dowling, she was set free. Helen Duncan died a few years later in 1956. Few today are able to duplicate her unique mediumship.

Other trance mediums even have the amazing ability to draw portraits of spirits. In England psychic artist Coral Polge accurately sketched the faces of spirits who contacted her. Over and over again, she drew pictures of loved ones who flocked her public demonstrations in England. Some who could not attend, such as Mrs. Baylesof Rhodesia, received portraits as well. Mrs. Bayles' son, who had died as a teenager during a routine operation, appeared to Coral Polge, who captured his likeness, much to his mother's delight. Her amazing story is told in her biography, *Living Images,* which was coauthored with Kay Hunter.

Recently, spirit artist Rev. Rita Berkowitz gave a workshop on spirit art at the New England School of Metaphysics. Rita, a medium and talented artist who coauthored of *The Idiot's Guide to Communicating With Spirits*, amazed the students with her perceptive descriptions of spirits. At the end of the seminar, she tuned into my grandfather without any prior knowledge of his appearance and personality. "This gentleman always wore a white shirt and a dark tie — he never liked coarse language," Rita explained as she deftly sketched this portrait of my grandfather, Harry Brickett. True, Grandpa, very protective of his "girls," never allowed any swearing in the house. He also always dressed in a white shirt, three-piece suit, and tie for his job at the Fiduciary Trust in Boston. The likeness (page 38) very much resembled my favorite picture of grandpa, which I placed in the dedication to the book.

Often mediums even pick up smells such as a whiff of tobacco or the scent of roses using clairgustance. Many times sitting in circle the scent of violets or roses can overwhelm the sitter and then just as suddenly disappear. Another phenomena is that of spirit touch. Some sitters feel like a helmet is on the their heads as spirit guides make contact. Often there is a light breeze when no window is opened or door ajar. American Indians pay attention to these changes in atmosphere as signs spirits are around. A good ghost hunter would be wise to follow suit.

Basically, ghosts are spirits still attached to the earth plane for some unfinished business. They will often visit their former homes or even places of business. Adelma Simmons' spirit is evident at her herb farm — Caprilands. Staff and visitors alike "feel" her attentive presence. You can almost hear her say, "That Shakespeare herb garden needs weeding." A medium would surely pick up the slender form of the elderly Mrs. Simmons sitting in the dining room, with a stack of beloved books piled high on the table by the window.

Professional ghost hunters such as Joshua P. Warren, author of *How to Hunt Ghosts,* prefer electronics to mediumship. Tape recorders, meters, and cameras are the tool of their trade. Taping the voices of spirits is not new. Even Thomas Edison believed that it would be possible someday to make a telephone to talk with the other side. Modern electronic voice phenomena began in 1959, when Swedish artist Friedrich Jürgenson recorded the voices of spirits on a reel-to-reel tape recorder. These voices conversed in several languages, giving messages such as "We are the dead — we live."

Hans Bender (a German parapsychologist) and Konstantin Raudive (a Latvian psychologist) both investigated the voices and felt them to be genuine. Raudive later published a book on his research, *Breakthrough,* which is based on the 72,000 spirit voices that he taped. In the 1980s, an American researcher, George Meek, invented Spiritcom, designed to allow two-way communication between this side of life and the next. Meek's book, *After We Die, Then What,* details his research in the world beyond.

In addition to tape recorders and even video-cameras, most ghost hunters rely on meters. Even a simple compass may be of assistance. A compass, for example, may be influenced by electromagnetic energy. Normally a compass points north, but if psychic intense electromagnetic activity is present, the needle may be all over the place, indicating paranormal activity. An even more sophisticated measuring device is the Electromagnetic Field Meter or EMF (page 65). Ghost hunter, Joshua Warren, recommends one that reads DC fields. However, an AC meter is acceptable. Apparently ghosts can change current. When using the EMF meter, look for an unusual reading where there is no source of electromagnetic activity, such as a TV or appliances.

Once a hot spot has been located, it is important to take a photograph. Often orbs, mists, and even the full outline or body of a spirit will appear. Psychic photography has been used successfully since 1862 when Boston photography William Mumler produced spirit photographs, known as thoughtography. One of his most famous clients was Mary Todd Lincoln. In Mrs. Lincoln's photo, the spirit of her deceased husband, Abraham Lincoln, appears — lovingly gazing over his widow's shoulder.

While full figures are known to crop up in photos, most psychic snapshots start with orbs. These orbs are reminiscent of the "spirit lights" mediums report. Orbs are round circle a few inches in diameters. As they form more fully, often the outline of a face can be detected. Sometime even a full face will appear with distinct features of the deceased spirit. Eventually the full body of the spirit can be seen. Whether in the form of orbs, mists, an outline or full figure, a spirit is there in full force during Spiritualist circles and especially during séances, when their presence is requested. At the New England School of Metaphysics, séances are the final test for the fledging mediums. Usually, I start séances by surrounding the séance circle with white light and then calling on spirits with an invocation such as:

> We call that which is for the highest good of each and ask that the loved ones, guides, and angels. Loving Father, Divine Mother: be present with us now.

In order to facilitate spirit communication, a glass of water is placed beside each sitter. Water is basically used as a conductor for ectoplasm. Often I can see hooded Franciscan monks assisting as well as my Hindu and Egyptian guides.

Shortly before the 2003 annual séance, I received a call from one of the students asking if she could take some pictures. "Sure," I said. "I will point out spirits for you as we go along." The student then sat opposite me with her camera poised. She began to randomly clicking the camera each time she felt compelled to do so. Trying to be of assistance, I moved around the room pointing at spirit lights toward the end of the séance, which lasted about an hour. She took twenty-six photos, and one captured what appear to be the hooded monks I saw protecting the group. The photograph is on page 38. Are spirits present? You be the judge.

In *Connecticut Ghosts,* mediumship combined with psychic photography and an EMF meter were the primary means for hunting ghosts. Many times, I would visit the home of spirits by invitation. Such was the case for the homes for Theodate Pope, William Gillette, and Adelma Simmons. Their spirits were most genial hosts — even they seem to enjoy visitors from the other side.

Other haunted houses, such as the Shaw Mansion in New London and Silas Dean's home in Wethersfield, I happened on "by chance." In the case of the Shaw residence, I stopped in only because the Eugene O'Neil cottage was closed for repairs. It turned out to be a very "hot" spot for spirit activity. As we toured the colonial mansion, the psychic energy was especially strong on the second floor where the family spent most of their time in the bedrooms and upstairs spacious landing where the Shaw family was known to gather for informal conversation and leisurely games. When I snapped a shot of the family area, I entered a portal in time and captured orbs of varying heights. It seems like a family of Shaw parents and children are still enjoying their New London home!

While the Shaw clan was happy to pose for a picture, many ghosts are suspicious of visitors. Unlike those in the flesh, ghosts will "sense" what you are up to. If ye be foe, watch out! It is always a good idea to be clear in your intention and ask spirit permission before you enter their realm. And don't forget to surround yourself with white light for protection!

Portrait of Harry Otis Brickett by Spirit Artist: Rev. Rita Berkowitz.

Were three hooded monks and a spirit guide really present in this photograph taken by one of the students attending the séance?

Chapter Four

Hartford's Haunted House

Hartford County has a checkered history with the occult. First, the colonists condemn to death as witches those who consulted with familiar spirits. Then, on the other hand, Victorians actively sought assistance from spirits. Its citizens are still divided on spirit communication. While some embrace New Age channelers, others still cast a cautious but curious eye on communicating with ghosts. For the most part, though, those who openly practice Wicca and Spiritualism are left alone. Few in the Hartford area notice that the Church of Divine Light, a Spiritualist church, meets every Sunday at 3:00 P.M. at the Unitarian Church in Hartford or that Rev Marie Langer, a Wiccan minister, can tell some great ghost stories of a small child playing ball in the church. Furthermore, she had the video to prove it!

Even the University of Connecticut takes a tolerant view of the paranormal. University of Connecticut professor Kenneth Ring did pioneer work in the near death experience in the 1970s. He researched people who had come close to dying but came back to tell of their experiences. Many reported separating from their body, and seeing the spirits of deceased relatives and beings of light. When they went toward the light, they were on the other side. Since it is not their time to go, relatives and guides appeared who told them it is not their time to die and they must return to the earth plane. Some, however, lingered long enough to go through a life review; others returned immediately. With continuing research into the near-death experience, it seems science is very close to proving the Spiritualist tenet: "There is no death and there are no dead."

With this knowledge in mind, my ghost hunting began. Using a tri-fold method: mediumship, psychic photography, and an Electromagnetic Field Meter, I set off to investigate Hartford County for ghosts. First, I made a tour of the Old New-Gate Prison in East Granby and the old colonial homes of Suffield adjacent to East Granby. Next, a visit to the historic section of old Wethersfield, then on to the Victorian homes of Mark Twain and Harriet Beecher Stowe, Katherine Seymor Day, and the Cheney Homestead in Manchester. Finally, I visited the Farmington home of famed architect, Theodate Pope. My first impression sitting on the grounds of Old New-Gate Prison on a beautiful July morning was one of gaiety — with sounds of almost raucous laughter. I was later to learn that that old colonial prison had once been used as a dance hall in the 1920s and later there was a small children's zoo on the grounds. The spot where I was sitting faced what once was the entrance to the dance hall. From the vibrations left behind, it must have been a speak-easy!

In any event, the atmosphere changed rapidly as my husband Ron and I entered the dark, damp copper mines. At first, it was a refreshing change from the hot sun. As we went deeper into the mines, there was a somber feeling — one of sadness and despair. The mines had been used as a prison during colonial times, and many a man felt the despair of the endless cycle of work. One poor prisoner decided to let an infection fester to avoid work. He developed gangrene and the desperate prisoner had to have his leg amputated. It was a "hard-rock" life for those incarcerated.

No wonder there was such a negative charge in the mines. Soon orbs of light began flashing. Deeper in the mines even more psychic energy was trapped. Spirit orbs were captured both on video and film. On page 50 is a picture of the orbs found in the dark caverns. As we left the mines, I said a few hasty prayers for the souls left behind.

The next town over from East Granby, Simsbury, has its share of paranormal activity. Simsbury's Pettibone Tavern, built in 1780 as a stagecoach stop for travelers from Boston to Albany, is said to be haunted by the ghost of a young woman, Abigail Pettibone. As legend has it, the young woman was murdered by her enraged husband. Apparently, her husband returned early from a whaling trip to find his wife in the arms of another man. In his rage, he is rumored to have murdered them both with an ax. Her family was so embarrassed by Abigail's adultery and subsequent murder that they removed her face from the family portrait, which now sits in the entryway of the tavern.

A few years back, when the Pettibone Tavern was still the Chart House, I made two trips to inspect its ghostly activity. The owner reported chairs being moved and staff feeling unearthly chills. Intrigued, I canvassed the building from attic to basement. To my surprise, there was quite a lot of psychic energy in the attic, which at one time was used to hide runaway slaves as a stop on the Underground Railroad. The original brick basement also held a lot of psychic energy. While we took photos of the interior, including Abigail's picture, no orbs appeared. However, Abigail was known to be flighty!

Just northeast of Simsbury is another lovely colonial town, Suffield. Tobacco is still one of its major industries, despite the fact that many of its farms have been turned into housing lots. Originally, the village was known as "south field" across the river from Enfield, the "end field." For many years, Suffield was home to some of the wealthiest families in Connecticut — the Alcorns, Hathaways, and Phelps. Two houses owned by prestigious Suffield citizens, the King House and the Hathaway House, are open to the public.

The Phelps-Hathaway House is an impressive white colonial house at 55 South Main Street. I have often attended craft fairs in the spacious barn and sensed the presence of familiar spirits. While the Phelps-Hathaway House is only open May through September, I was able to walk around the grounds and was drawn to the barn area. I sensed spirit activity there, but alas none of the energy was captured on film.

A few blocks north of the King and Hathaway houses is the historic First Congregation Church of Suffield. Reverend Ebenezer Gay (1718-1796), a graduate of Harvard, was its third minister. His sermons preserved both the religious sentiments and the history of the town. Since he and his wife had no children, they cared for several black children, including two girls named "Sarah" and "Ti." The historic church has also been the site of some spirit activity. One church member, "Robin," has even taken pictures overshadowed with ghostly mists in the church basement. While visiting the Hathaway House, I stopped and took some photographs of the old graveyard in back of the church. As you can see from the photos on page 51, it was a cold March day with little spirit activity.

Next, I made a leisurely trip down Route 91 to another colonial town, Wethersfield, and the home of Silas Deane. Deane, a wealthy merchant, had a great deal of pride. Born into humble circumstances as the son of a blacksmith, Silas Deane studied law at Yale University. Later he married a wealthy widow. During the Revolutionary War, he was sent to France along with Benjamin Franklin and Arthur Lee to procure supplies for the Continental Army. However, Lee accused Deane of making a profit in the insurance industry by using insider information, and in 1778 Lee testified against Deane before Congress.

Sadly, Deane was to spend the rest of his life and what was left his fortune trying to regain his honor. On his return to America via the Boston Packet, Deane became suddenly ill and died. Impressed by Silas Deane's determination to clear his name at all cost, I thought, "Now that is a man I would enjoy meeting." Impulsively, I took a picture of Silas Deane, as I looked at his portrait in the parlor of the Silas Deane House in Wethersfield. When the photographs of the visit there developed, only one showed an orb — near the portrait of Silas Deane. By the way, recent scholarship suggests that Deane may have been the victim of a double-cross, as his "friend" Doctor Bancorft "an expert in South American poison" was also a British spy.[1]

Towns continued to prosper in Connecticut. Just across the Connecticut River from Wethersfield, farmers such as Timothy Cheney of Manchester made their fortunes in the rich Connecticut soil. Later, their sons turned to manufacturing. In the 1800s the Cheney brothers made millions with the manufacture of silk. Tim Cheney was also known for making fine clocks and his grandsons, Seth and John, were well-known artists. The Cheney Homestead, built in 1785, is open to the public. Located at 106 Hartford Road, it retains much of its original character. A picture of Lake Pepin by Seth Cheney and a tall clock is seen on the face of Timothy Cheney's built-in clock. In the upstairs parlor, which was used by the family as an informal sitting room, a beautiful portrait of Spiritualist Katherine Fox in her prime graces the wall. The striking brunette likeness of the talented medium seems to preside over the room, which was once used for family séances. Orbs of magnetic energy flew around the room, as if to draw attention to the portrait and round table in the center of the room. Whatever séances took place here, there is no doubt that they were the "real deal."

Next, a trip to Nook Farm in Hartford brought us back to Mark Twain's day, when Hartford was a flourishing community with many publishing companies lining Farmington Avenue. Nook Farm is a cozy community in which housed Mark Twain, Harriet Beecher Stowe, and Katherine Seymour Day. Of their three homes, two hot spots were found — one in the dining room of the Beecher-Stow house and in second in the Day home parlor. Both seem to still have much psychic energy. No hot spots were found in the home of Mark Twain, who was at best ambivalent about spirit communication.

The Beecher-Stowe house brings visitors back in time to the life of the Victorian lady. Harriet Beecher-Stowe had a keen interest in her kitchen, designing many practical innovations such as flour bins in the kitchen rather than in an adjacent pantry. This made for easy access. Her home is that of the sensible Victorian woman who wrote *Uncle Tom's Cabin*. Harriet Beecher-Stowe did most of her writing in her second-story bedroom, which faces the backyard, on a lady's writing desk. Just to the right of the desk within an easy glance is a homemade picture of her daughter framed in a sunflower. Her children were never far from her thoughts.

Both she and her husband, Calvin, were devoted parents who lost one son as a small child. Later, their son, Henry, a college student at Trinity College died; both his parents were devastated by Henry's death, so much so that they tried to contact their dead sons. After Henry Stowe died, Harriet consulted a powerful medium in Italy who communicated "strong impressions from the spirit world, so that I often feel sustained and comforted, as if I had been near my Henry and other departed friends."[1]

Harriet and her husband were known to hold séances in their home. While Harriet's spiritual energy is strong by her writing desk, the most charged room in the home seems to be the dining room. As I entered the room, I felt a distinct psychic charge and soon saw orbs flitting around. "This must have been where Harriet Beecher-Stowe conducted table-tipping and séances. The large oval dining table would be a perfect spot to place fingertips, and wood is an excellent conductor of spiritual energy," I thought.

As I left the house and toured the garden two beautiful blue butterflies flying in tandem greeted me. Usually butterflies just pass by, but these two remained close while I was walking though the garden. Each magnificent butterfly flew parallel to the other late in the afternoon. The two blue butterflies, symbols of the eternal life that Calvin and Harriet ardently adhered to, seemed a perfect end to a lovely summer day. As I reluctantly walked away from the garden, I thought, "The Beecher-Stowe house is definitely the home of a believer."

A much lighter, more social energy is felt in the grander home of her neighbor Mark Twain. After all, he was known to poke fun at spirits. Not so much Twain's energy was felt in the vast entryway of the house Twain patterned after a river boat, but that of his daughter, Susie, who died in the house. Clairvoyantly, I spied her and two other ladies sitting politely on the round settee that faces the front door. They said not a word, but smiled to greet visitors. Other than this spirit welcoming committee, little psychic energy seemed present in the house.

The house, of course, is filled with Twain's whimsy. Just to the left of the settee is a telephone booth housing one of the area's first telephones. On the second floor is Mark Twain's bedroom, which is dominated by an elegant Italian bed with an ornately carved headboard. Twain slept facing the headboard. He joked it was so expensive he wanted to look at it. The top floor housed Twain's domain — his billiard room where he did much as his writing. I suspect that if the spirit of Mark Twain was still with us that would be where a visitor would most likely find him.

The final stop on the Nook Farm tour was the home of Katherine Seymour Day, the niece of Harriet Beecher Stowe and granddaughter of her sister, Isabella Hooker Beecher. The energy had a mixed feeling of the many who visited the library upstairs, but as I entered the parlor I noticed the sunflower design etched around the rim of the fireplace mantel. "Another believer, I thought, as the sunflower is the flower of Spiritualism." Next, as if to confirm my thoughts, I saw an orb flitting over Katherine Seymour Day's picture sitting on the mantel in the room next door.

About a twenty minute drive from Nook Farm is the Hill-Stead Museum, the home of architect Theodate Pope Riddle. Many in Connecticut recognize her as the designer and patroness of Avon Old Farms School, but few realize she generously subsidized studies in parapsychology. According to Sandra Katz, author of Riddle's biography, *Dearest of Genius*, Riddle's interest in parapsychology was not just a passing fancy. She funded research headed by William James. James, author of *Varieties of Religious Experience,* worked with medium Leonora Piper. Through Mrs. Piper, she often communicated with the spirit of Dr. Richard Hodgson, who seemed aware of everything that was happening to Theo, including a recent fire at Hill-Stead that had burned down the stable. His said that he prayed that the fire might not spread and assured Theo that the little dog that had died in the fire was with him in the spiritual world.[2]

She was also known to invite mediums to Hill-Stead, both William James and his brother, the celebrated author Henry James, were houseguests. Often she would travel to New York to visit the New York Society for Psychical Research. One of her dreams was to establish such a society in Connecticut. In fact, she and her maid were on a mission to visit the British Society for Psychical Research in London on the ill-fated ship *Lusitania* a year before her marriage. As fate would have it, she survived the ship's sinking, but just barely. In a sea strewn with the dead, Theodate Pope drifted in and out of consciousness, managing to float on her back until she spotted an oar, which she clung to for several hours. Somehow the oar had slid under her heavy skirts, which were weighing her down, and acted as buoy to keep her afloat while she drifted, semi-conscious. Eventually, she became the last survivor to be picked up by the up by the rescue ship, the *Julia*.[3]

Theodate's life was full of other surprises. For example, she reported having an out of body experience at age nine. Apparently, she was gazing at her reflection in a mirror and the next thing she knew, she was looking at herself from the outside with the thought, "This body isn't me."[4] At twenty-two, she surprised many by becoming an architect at a time when women of a certain class were not expected to enter into a career. When her dearest friend, Mary Hillard's brother died from influenza at age twenty-six, she turned to Spiritualism at the urging of another close friend, artist Mary Cassatt. Later, at forty-nine, just as most people assumed she would never marry, she accepted John Wallace Riddle's proposal .She even took in three foster boys in her later years, the first of whom, Gordon, died at age four.

Her residence, Hill-Stead House, which she designed and built for her parents at the turn of the twentieth century in Farmington is a thirty-room Colonial Revival "farmhouse." While most of the furnishings and paintings were chosen by her parents, the library reflects Theodate's taste in reading. Its shelves house a first class collection of books on parapsychology and the major world religions. Hill-Stead in suburban Farmington was quite rural when it was built. Theodate Pope Riddle encouraged self-sufficiency and farming. She even had a pet cow, Anastacia. Her home, Hill-Stead House, is a tribute to the woman who dearly loved her home, yet had a passion for travel and loved to collect, much like her father Alfred Pope, a millionaire who made his fortune in malleable steel. However, unlike her father, who collected Monet, Manet, and Whistler, Theodate Pope Riddle believed such a priceless collection should be housed in a museum rather than a private collection. At her death, August 3, 1946, she left Hill-Stead House as a museum, with a private trust to maintain the magnificent estate. Should Hill-Stead fail, the money would go to her second love, Avon Old Farms School for Boys.

Theodate Pope Riddle's generous spirit was very much in evidence the day I placed the call to Hill-Stead, requesting permission to photograph the interior. After I left a voice mail for the curator, I felt the spirit of Theodate Pope Riddle tap me on my shoulder while I was leisurely sipping ice tea on my sun porch. A genteel spirit voice followed with the words, "Your wish will be granted."

Sure enough, I was given permission to photograph Hill-Stead's rooms. During the September visit that ensued, I felt the strongest energy in the library and again in the back room, which had once been her father's study, but was later used as a morning room for Theodate Pope Riddle. As I toured the elegant mansion, I was struck by the round table in the living room. Could it have been used for a séance in the 1920s? When we visited her library I felt her spirit pull me to a golden-tan silk chair next to small table with her picture on it. The energy was tremendous, as if Theodate Pope Riddle was sitting there waiting to greet visitors. Next, I was pulled to a particular section of the vast library. I looked up and saw row upon row of books on parapsychology by well-known authors such as Frederic Myers and William James. Since I had not yet researched her life, I was surprised at the quality and size of the collection.

While we did photograph one orb on the second floor, intuitively I felt Theodate Pope Riddle wanted us to return. In November, I brought an EMF meter, a bottle of water (a spirit conductor), and a parapsychology student, Maureen Forrester. However, initially, our investigation seemed futile. Cynthia Cormier, the museum's curator and our tour guide, seemed genuinely interested with the paranormal. Throughout the investigation, I remained silent, not wishing to influence Maureen. However, she soon was seeing orbs in the library. While in the library, one of the caretakers joined us. Soon he was telling us how he had heard spirit voices while working in the house. With Maureen, Cynthia, and now an additional staff person joining our group, the whole atmosphere seemed conducive to parapsychology investigation.

As a group we entered Theodate Pope Riddle's study at to the back of the estate. While the EMF meter registered some energy by Pope's tan velvet chair in the library (a four out of a possible ten), it seemed to suddenly turn upward as I approached her desk. The strongest reading came from a picture strategically placed facing the room. "Who is this man?," I asked Cynthia. "That is Henry James, " she answered. "Was he related to William James?" "Yes, they were bothers. Both visited Hill-Stead," replied our tour guide. Remembering the dream I had had of William James the previous night, I realized who our spirit guide was.

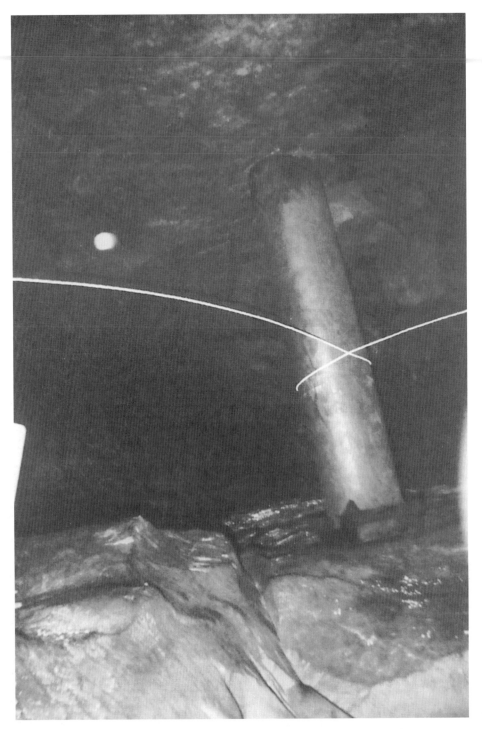

Orbs in the mines at Old New-Gate Prison. *Photographer: Elaine Kuzmeskus*

Webb House. *Photographer: Elaine Kuzmeskus*

Phelps-Hathaway House in Suffield. *Photographer: Elaine Kuzmeskus*

In this picture of the Mark Twain House, it almost looks like someone is looking out the window from the empty upstairs bedroom! *Photographer: Elaine Kuzmekus*

Harriet Beecher-Stowe's house in Hartford is definitely the home of a believer. *Photographer: Elaine Kuzmeskus*

A mist that materialized over the portrait of
Theodate Pope Riddle. *Photographer: Elaine
Kuzmeskus*

Theodate Pope Riddle, Farmington architect who wished to establish a society for psychical research in Connecticut. *Archives, Hill-Stead Museum, Farmington, CT.*

Portrait of Abigail Pettibone. Notice that her face had been cut out of the picture because she disgraced her family and later painted back in. *Photographer: Elaine Kuzmeskus*

Directions

Cheney Homestead
106 Hartford Road
Manchester, CT 06040
Telephone: (860) 645-5588
From Hartford: Take 84 East to 384 East. Then take 384 East to Exit 3. Turn right on Route 85 South (Main Street). Then left onto Hartford Road.

Harriet Beecher Stowe House
77 Forest Street
Hartford, CT 06105
Telephone: (860) 522-9258

Hill-Stead Museum
35 Mountain Road
Farmington, CT 06032
Telephone: (860)677-4787
From Hartford: Take Route 84 East to Exit 39. Continue straight onto Route 4 West. Turn left onto Route 10 South (Main Street). At the light, turn left onto Mountain Road.

Mark Twain House and Museum
351 Farmington Avenue
Hartford, CT 06105
Telephone (860) 522-9258

Old New-Gate Prison From Hartford
Newgate Road
East Granby, CT 06035
From Hartford: Take Route 91 North to Exit 40 to Route 20 East
and follow the signs to Old New-Gate Prison.

Pettibone Tavern
4 Hartford Road
Simsbury, CT 06070
From Hartford: Take 91 to Route 20 East to Route 10 in
Simsbury.

Phelps-Hathaway House
55 South Main Street (Route 75)
Suffield, CT 06078
Telephone: (860) 668-0373
From Hartford: Take 91 North to Exit 40. Then take Route 75
North for approximately four miles. The Hathaway House is on
your left.

Webb-Deane-Stevens Museum
211 Main Street
Wethersfield, CT 06109
Telephone: (860) 529-0612
From Hartford: Take 91 North to Old Wethersfield exit. Take a
right onto Great Meadow Road. Next, a left onto Marsh Street.
Then take a left onto Main Street.

Chapter Five

Strange Happenings in Fairfield

"Hungry ghosts" the Buddhists call them, spirits that are driven by very human desires: addictions, greed, and revenge. They haunt taverns and disaster sites. Some spirits don't even know they are dead. Fairfield, the wealthiest county in Connecticut, has had its share of strange happenings: poltergeist activity at Phelps Mansion in Stratford, non-registered ghosts at the Red Brook Inn in Mystic, strange lights at the Union Cemetery in Easton, and The Lady in White who has been seen by visitors to Our Lady of the Rosary Cemetery in Monroe.

One of the most documented cases of poltergeist activity began in March of 1850 at the Phelps Mansion on Elm Street in Stratford. The mansion, built by sea captain George Dowell, was designed with a seventy-foot-long main hallway and twin staircases, not unlike the layout of Captain Dowell's clipper ship. When Rev. Eliakim Phelps bought the mansion in 1848 he was a widower looking to make some changes in his life. Not only was he a well-known Christian minister, but he was also interested in mesmerism and the newly formed Spiritualist movement. He was also interested in getting married again, and soon he married a young woman with three children, ages sixteen to six. Later, they had a son of their own, Henry.

Yet all was not well in the Phelps household. Apparently Mrs. Phelps and her daughter were unhappy. The events, however, of March 10 only made matters worse. When the family returned from church, they discovered all the doors of the house had been flung open, despite the fact that the entire house had been locked before they left and the only keys were in Rev. Phelps's pocket!

Later in the day, when the rest of the family was out of the house, Rev Phelps hid in his study to protect himself against any more intruders. Soon his of mind was disturbed. According to researcher Troy Taylor, "He [Rev. Phelps] opened the door to the dining room and got a shocking discovery. The previously empty room was now filled with a crowd of women."[1] Somehow they had entered without permission and remained in the room kneeling in prayer.

The "spirits" turned out to be dummies created by invisible hands from dresses stuffed with rags. Apparently, the supernatural forces were having a field day at the Phelps's residence. Over the ensuing month about twenty spirit women mysteriously appeared to Dr. Phelps. According to author Joseph Citro, the Phelps's youngest child saw the figures as well. When he entered the room he saw a "figure" wearing a dress belonging to Mrs. Phelps kneeling in prayer. The child whispered, "Be still Ma is saying her prayers."

Soon the happenings at the Phelps Mansion became the talk of Stratford. Furniture, food, china, books, pens, a small knife, and an umbrella flew through the air. Even a heavy marble-topped table suddenly levitated off the ground and smashed to the floor. In April 1850, a reporter from the *New York Sun* witnessed unseen forces claw at daughter Anna's arms. Rolling back Anna's sleeve, the reporter observed horrific red marks. Several people witnessed the youngest son levitated from his bed by invisible forces, which then him dumped on the floor. By October, nearly all the windows in the home were broken by objects flying through the air.

What in the world was going on? Ghosts? A vision? Or was colonial Stratford witch, Goody Bassett, getting her revenge?

Many locals believed it was the latter. After all, Goody Bassett was hanged for witchcraft in 1651 from a tree near the house. Others, including Spiritualist minister Andrew Jackson Davis, believed some of the members of the Phelps household were psychic. When the well-known author and Spiritualist minister visited the home, he attributed the poltergeist activity to "vital radiations," a kind of electricity from family members that caused the objects to fly in the air. Another minister, Rev John Mitchell, actually communicated with the spirits present using rapping as a code. One spirit even requested a glass of gin. When asked why these events were occurring, the spirit simply tapped out "for fun."[2]

In the 1970s the house became a nursing home. Soon after the opening, staff began to complain of poltergeist activity. Ed and Lorraine Warren, famed psychic investigators, were called in. However, the Warrens were unable to find a source for the disturbances. Before long the building caught fire and was abandoned. Modern investigators may never know for sure what caused the paranormal activity at 1738 Elm Street as the Phelp's Mansion was leveled to make room for a housing complex just outside the American Shakespeare Theatre.

Revenge, however, does seem to be the motive behind a strange incident at the Red Brook Inn in Mystic around the 1960s. John Jones (fictional name), the owner of the Crary House (later to be renamed the Red Brook Inn), thought he would never be caught when he began a love affair with his wife's best friend. When his wife Mary did find out about the affair between the two, she was livid at the double betrayal. Her husband swore to be true. Later, when Mary contracted cancer, both her husband and her best friend nursed her. Under their care, Mary lived another twelve years. When Mary died, John promptly moved out and married his mistress, "Jane."

Later the Crary House was sold and turned into the Red Brook Inn. Jane decided the inn would be the perfect spot to celebrate her husband's eightieth birthday. Mary, now in spirit, considered the party to be in poor taste and as soon as the party began a foul odor till the room. If that wasn't ghostly enough, as John went to cut the first slice of his birthday cake, the cake just disintegrated into bits and pieces. Was it Mary having her revenge? According to innkeeper, Ruth Orr, "It's impossible for a carrot cake to fall apart like that."

There have been other ghostly presences at the Red Brook Inn. One ghost is credited with saving the lives of occupants of Room Two. The spirit of an elderly white-haired lady was seen on two occasions. In one incident, twenty-seven-year-old Christopher Campbell was awakened by the elderly female ghost. He quickly realized the room was filled with smoke as the flue the fireplace was closed. The white-haired spirit appeared again in March of 1986. John Clodig, an organist, was awakened by an elderly woman. Again, the room was filled with smoke due to a closed flue.

Not only are residences — both private and public – subject to haunting, but places where the dead are buried are often sites of paranormal activity. Fairfield County has two well-known haunted cemeteries: Union Cemetery in Easton and Our Lady of the Rosary in Monroe. Union Cemetery, located on the corner of Routes 59 and 136, has gravestones dating back to the 1600s. There are tales of a caretaker's spirit being sighted there. Apparently, the caretaker became so obsessed with the 200-year-old spirit of a fur-trapper that, when he died, his ghost stayed on to guard the wrought iron fence of Union Cemetery, according to the Cosmic Society. The society also reports sightings of uniformed ghosts. When asked, "Where are you going?" the spirit soldiers answer "Straight through."[3] The Union Cemetery has also been the site of a female ghost known simply as the "Lady in

White" for over eighty years. Other spirit sightings of a mysterious lady in white have taken place in Our Lady of the Rosary Church in Monroe, twenty-three miles away.

Intrigued by the "Lady in White," I decided to take a crew to both cemeteries to investigate. On January 13, 2005, Dr. Susan Roberts, her assistant, Richard Doak, and I explored Union Cemetery in Easton and Our Lady of the Rosary Cemetery in Monroe. The day was unseasonably warm and foggy with mists generated by the melting snow. We brought two cameras (one "throwaway" and one digital), an EMF meter, and boots to navigate the cemeteries still covered with two feet of snow.

Dr Roberts operated the EMF meter as I clairvoyantly scanned the grounds of Union Cemetery. The meter never moved above a one. However, as I clairvoyantly canvassed the small cemetery, I saw many protective spirit lights surrounding it. Richard Doak captured some of this phenomena on his digital camera. As you can see from the photos on page 65, there were indeed many spirits present that day.

We had quite a time finding Monroe. When we finally arrived at Our Lady of the Rosary Cemetery, we began our investigation with the EMF meter. The meter was at a steady one until Dr. Roberts pointed it toward the woods and it spike up to a two. The woods are the exact spot where the Lady in White is supposed to appear. Sensing little activity and a bit disappointed, we headed back to the car. However, as we approached the black wrought iron gates on our way out, the EMF meter jumped to seven and then eight. Richard took pictures (page65) near the gate where the EMF meter indicated electromagnetic energy. While we did not meet the white lady, we did find both cemeteries hot spots for paranormal activity. As the crew left off for Monroe, I sense that the van was filled not only with three people and equipment, but also with a warm vibration and sense of peace, which to me always signals with presence of spirit helpers.

Curious to find the identities of our hitchhikers, I started to tune in to the spirits as I navigated Route 25. "Susan, " I called to the back seat. "Try the meter as I say their names – Rev. Dorothy Smith." "The meter's a ten," Dr. Roberts noted. I smiled, for the late Dorothy Smith was the Spiritualist pastor of the Albertson Memorial Church in Old Greenwich who passed over in 2003. "Guess she still has a sense of adventure," I commented. Next, remembering the man I considered our best modern trance medium, who died two years before Rev. Smith, I asked, "How about Elwood Babbitt?" "The meter is going crazy again – ten," answered Dr Roberts. Sure enough, when the crew developed their photos, spirits were very much present, with a little help from spiritual colleagues!

Photograph of the Red Brook Inn, Mystic, Connecticut. *Photographer: Marianne Alibozak*

Electromagnetic Field Meter. *Photographer: Richard Doak Jr.*

Orbs at Union Cemetery, Easton, CT. *Photographer: Richard Doak Jr.*

Orbs surrounding Union Cemetery, Easton, CT. *Photographer: Richard Doak, Jr.*

Addresses

Our Lady of the Rosary
Pepper Street (off Route 25)
Monroe, CT 06468
Telephone: (203) 261-8290
Directions from Hartford: Take Route 84 West to CT 34 - Exit 11.
Turn right on Mile Hill Road. Next, turn right onto Berkshire
Road. Then a slight right onto Toddy Hill Road which becomes
Bostsford Hill Road. Turn left on Main Street (25 South) and a
slight left onto Pepper Street.

Red Brook Inn
2750 Gold Star Highway
Old Mystic, CT 06372
Telephone (203)572-0349
Directions from Hartford: Take Route 91 South to 95 South to
Exit 90 — Old Mystic.

Union Cemetery
Junction of Highway 59 and Highway 136
(Near the Easton Baptist Church)
Easton, CT 06612
Telephone: (203) 375-4932
Directions from Hartford: Take Route 91 South to Exit 17 -
Route 15 and take Exit 46 to Route 59.

Chapter Six

Litchfield County — The Most Haunted Town in the United States

Litchfield County is known for its fine fly fishing in the Housatonic River, a picturesque covered bridge in Cornwall, and the most haunted town in the United States — Dudleytown. Dudleytown has been called the most haunted town in Connecticut with good reason. Strange maladies, murders, insanity, and suicides have plagued this rural town since its inceptions in 1730 — not what one would expect in this quiet northwest corner of Connecticut.

Dudleytown was founded by Thomas Grifis in 1739. Thirty-five years later, in August 1774, a strange illness came to town and Adoniram Cater infected his whole immediate family — all of whom died. His brother, Nathaniel, fled with his wife and children to neighboring New York. His troubles followed him; Nathaniel, his wife, and infant were killed by hostile Indians. His other three children were taken hostage by the Indians. Only his son, David Carter, who married an Indian woman, escaped the curse.

Later, Revolutionary War General Herman Swife's wife, Sarah, was struck by lightning. The town folks felt the general, one of Dudleytown's most celebrated citizens, became "slightly demented." Soon the general was found aimlessly wandering around the town, driven mad by his wife's cruel demise. Another husband, John Patrick Brophy, lost his wife and sanity in the town in the late 1800s. She died of consumption and grief after their children disappeared. Later, when the Brophy home was destroyed by fire, locals believed John Brophy had gone made and started the fire himself.[1]

Some folks felt the bad luck might be due to the Indians. Perhaps an unsuspecting settler had built over an Indian burial ground. Rev. Gary Dudley believes the "ghosts" could even have been a figment of imagination caused by a mold in rye, ergot. Other citizens of Dudleytown blame the town's woes on the three Dudley brothers who settled the area. According to local legend, the three brothers were related to an Englishman, Edward Dudley, who had tried to kill Henry VIII. Could the English monarchy have put a curse on the Dudley family for plotting to kill their king?

While the source of the gloom that surrounded Dudleytown is unclear, many settlers, fearing further disasters, fled the town. By 1899 Dudleytown had become a ghost town. People who later visited the area reported eerie energy and observed the area had become a negative zone, where no hoofed animals were to be found within its boundaries.

However, that didn't stop Dr William Carter, a New York City cancer specialist, from building a vacation home in Dudleytown. He simply wanted a quiet place to summer with his children and grandchildren. Not one to be superstitious, the good doctor left his wife for two days to tend to an emergency in a neighboring town. When he returned, he discovered his wife in a state of abject fear. She had gone mad. The couple quickly left their vacation home, hoping a return to their residence would sooth Mrs. Carter's frayed nerves. However, she was too far into her psychotic world to improve. Sadly, two weeks later, Mrs. Carter committed suicide. Thus, the legend of Dudleytown was born.

Today, ghost hunters, Spiritualists, Wiccans, and the curious make the trek to Litchfield County to experience the dead zone for themselves. So many trekkers came that the selectmen voted to change the name of Dudleytown Road to Bear Mountain Road. Don't bother to ask directions from the locals, as they are also likely to deceive you. If you are fortunate enough to actually locate Dudleytown, remember not to go alone. At the very least, you will need a second person to wait in the car as you explore. The area is posted with multiple signs which state, "Parked cars will be towed per order of the selectmen." Those who trespass or park illegally can be fined $75 per person.

On a bright June day the crew — my husband, Ron and myself and our spirit guides — set out to find Dudleytown. After a false start when a local businessman directed us to the opposite side of town, we located a more friendly citizen who explained Dudleytown Road was now Bear Mountain Road about five mile west.

As we turned into Bear Mountain Road, my stomach started to churn with apprehension. It wasn't long before Ron felt negative vibes on the back of his neck. We unloaded the cameras and tool to take some still pictures, without much success. "I am going into the old area of the town," Ron said. "Be careful," I warned and returned to our green Suburban to wait — and pray.

Was Dudleytown a dead zone? Are the ancient cellar holes and walls still haunted? When Ron returned he confirmed that there was a negative charge to the energy and an eerie stillness. Nowhere did he see any wildlife. While our trip with medium, meter, and cameras didn't produce any psychic photographs, clairvoyant investigation confirmed the negative charge in the area, which I sensed extended about five feet in all directions. Whether we were on an old Indian burial ground or surrounded by tortured spirits who had died in the area, it was not a pleasant sensation.

The unsettled feeling continued to surround us, causing irritation in the stomach and apprehension. On the verge of a quarrel, we left the area, planning to return when we both were in better spirits. It wasn't until we reached the banks of the Houstonic River — five mile past Dudleytown — that a charge of positive energy greeted us, as I clairvoyantly saw the spirits of the ancient Indians walking protectively along its banks. Perhaps a second trip would have yielded more evidence of paranormal activity. However, one trip to Dudleytown was enough for me!

Celestine Smith of New Haven agrees, many who go to Dudleytown can feel the evil there, "It's an interesting place, but I wouldn't want to go there." According to Smith, a couple who recently went camping at Dudleytown with another couple, returned home with tragic results. The wife, the more sensitive of the two, started hearing voices telling her that her husband was cheating on her. Despite her bewildered husband's protest of innocence, his wife filed for divorce. Bt the way, the Internet is filled with stories of break-up, illnesses, and accidents experienced by those who visit Dudleytown. Whether such events are due to a curse or negative spirits, it is best to tread lightly on Dudleytown's soil.

According to the Tao, wherever there is great negative energy, great spiritual energy is present to balance. Hence the Chinese circular yin-yang symbol — half white with a dot of black and half black with a spot of white. While Litchfield County is host to the most haunted town in the United States, it is also home to a most spiritual Meditation center — the Woodbury Yoga Center.

While you are exploring the occult in Litchfield County, don't overlook this yoga center, where the spirit of the late Dhyanyogi Mahusadandas is very much present. As the story goes, the Dhyanyogi while on his deathbed in India was called back by a vision of Western devotees beckoning him back to life. Fortunately, the Danyogi recovered and toured the United States, where he met and inspired Janiki Pierson to found the Woodbury Yoga center on property donated by her mother. I have visited the Woodbury Yoga Center many times and have found the Spirit of Danyogi kept alive by his successor, Shri Anandi Ma, and the many who practice meditation there.

The best time to visit is when Shri Anandi Ma is present. Her meditation in the great hall is very enlightening. Once, during a four-day retreat, I felt the shakti power rise so forcefully that my neck began to vibrate. Unable to control these forceful emanations, I moved to a spot at the back of the meditation hall to brace myself against the wall. Later, I learned that these emanations were helpful kundalini energy — clearing the throat chakra.

Dudleytown is not the friendliest spot. *Photographer: Elaine Kuzmeskus*

The woods at Dudleytown have an strange silence. *Photographer: Ronald Kuzmeskus*

Addresses

Dudleytown
Bald Mountain Road
Cornwall, CT
Directions from Hartford: Take Route 84 West to CT Route 4 to
Cornwall.

Woodbury Yoga Center
122 West Side Road
Woodbury, CT 06798
Telephone: (203) 263-2254
Directions from Hartford: Take Route 84 West to CT Route 64
South to Route 6 South and go right onto Route 317. Go one
mile and take a right onto West Side Road.

Chapter Seven

The Spirit of Middlesex

"William Gillett loved his cats — he would even hold birthday parties for them on his boat, *Aunt Polly*," explained the tour guide at Gillette Castle when asked about the many feline details throughout the castle. Her explanation confirmed my view of the famous Connecticut resident. "Whimsical, colorful, and eccentric" are adjectives that come to mind when I envision William Gillette, the actor who became famous playing the role of Sherlock Holmes on stage. In 1919, after a successful stage career, William Gillette retired to East Haddam, Connecticut, where he purchased 184 acres of land on which he designed and built a replica of a medieval castle, filled with Impressionist paintings and innovative built-in couches. To complete his retreat, Gillette added a private railroad and a houseboat.

A descendant of Thomas Hooker, Hartford's founding father on his mother's side, William Hooker Gillette was accustomed to elegant living at Nook Farm, with next door neighbors of Mark Twain and Harriet Beecher Stowe. Originally, the Gillette's heralded from France, arriving in Connecticut in the 1600s. His father, a senator and wealthy farmer, wanted the youngest of his three sons to be a lawyer. However, Mark Twain, another citizen of Hartford, encouraged the youthful William Gillette in his aspirations for the stage. It was with great sadness that Senator Francis Gillette put his son on a New York bound train when William Gillette decided to seek his fortune in the theatre.

Success was slow in developing. Even though Gillette had attended Trinity, Yale, Harvard, and Massachusetts Institute of Technology, he never received a degree. His first recognition as an actor came when Gillette stood in for the lead all in *Broken Hearts* at the Boston Museum. This led to better roles such as that of Sherlock Holmes, which he honed to perfection. In fact, Basil Rathbone based his portrayal of Holmes on Gillette's. In addition to his enormous success as Sherlock Holmes, Gillette invented many trick stage props and wrote two novels. After his semi-retirement in 1910, Gillette went on to do four revival tours. In 1919, William Gillette designed and built his retirement castle, giving his last performance at the Bushnell in 1936, the year before his death.

Did Gillette share with Sir Arthur Connan-Doyle, creator of Sherlock Holmes, a belief in spirit communication? While Gillette's views on Spiritualism are unknown, his love of the theatre was legendary. From a distance, his home looks like a medieval castle (page 80). He also had a flair for invention. His castle's furnishings include built-in couches, a movable table on tracks, and light switches of uniquely carved wood. One room which puzzles many is the hidden room in the middle of the castle. Was it used for romantic trysts or as a hideout from frequent guests? Or was it a place of safekeeping? Perhaps even a place of retreat or mediation — even a séance room? We shall never know for sure, as William Gillette took the secret to his grave. However, there were several spirits present during our visit on a lovely late August afternoon. On page 80 is a picture showing an orb indicative of the protective spirit of perhaps William Gillette himself or his Japanese housekeeper.

Next, on our tour of Middlesex County is the Goodspeed Opera House, also in East Haddam. Built in 1876, the six-story Opera House was built by William Goodspeed, a ship builder. Facing the banks of the Connecticut River, it was designed to attract the attention of the river traffic of the day (page 81). It is just as picturesque today, with its spacious grounds of the riverbank making a lovely spot for an afternoon picnic.

Visiting the Opera House on a bright August afternoon, I was reminded of the Halloween in 1997 when I conducted a séance at midnight — following the play *Metamorphosis* based on the life of Harry Houdini. I am frequently asked, "Did Houdini really come through?" You be the judge.

Promptly at midnight, the official Houdini Séance began on stage with several participants around a round oak table. I was at the head, facing the audience and the assistant medium, Barbara Dresden-Masse, was seated opposite me. Other members of the inner circle were as follows: Sidney Radner, the séance director; Thomas Built, President of the Houdini Historical Society; Dr. Morris Young, magic historian; Geno Muntari, owner of Houdini's in Las Vegas; John Gaughan, illusion designer; Gene Camache, from Coyote Productions, producer of documentary film, *Houdini*; Tony Wild, coauthor of a *Houdini* screenplay; Larry Weeks, Houdini historian; Anna Crankshaw, great granddaughter of Margery Cransdon; and the actors Timothy Gulan, who played Houdini and Lewis Cleale, who played Theo, Houdini's brother in *Metamorphosis*. This was quite an impressive group.

Not surprisingly, Barbara and I seemed to be the most earnest seekers. However, I just focused even more intently to bring up the vibrations. Messages came through for those present at the séance table. When I came to Timothy Gulan, the young actor who portrayed Houdini in the play, Houdini did indeed have a message! I told the actor, "I have been around to help you with the magic tricks in the play — many of which are difficult for you. In fact a few weeks ago when you injured your shoulder and decided not to go that evening, I urged you to continue and do the play, which you did." He then encouraged the actor to persevere in his career. He also added that with some changes the play had a shot at Broadway. Timothy Gulan did agree that the personal message from Houdini had been an accurate one. He had indeed felt a "presence" when he was attempting to learn magic tricks, which he had never studied before, and two weeks before he injured his shoulder doing one of the tricks and planned to cancel the performance. However, he felt strongly he should go on, which he did. Houdini had comments about the play as well. He felt it was too long and the humor needed a lot of work.

Do I think Houdini came through? Yes, I believe his spirit was present that evening. In fact, Houdini's spirit dressed in an elegant 1920s tuxedo appeared in my bedroom two days before the event to reassure me he was planning to attend the séance. Also, his message for Timothy Gulan was evidential. It would have been characteristic of the childless magician, who was fond of young people, to reach out to the young actor. However, the official test of the séance to prove Harry Houdini was present was to have the great magician from spirit open the handcuffs placed in front of me. Since this had not occurred at this or any of the Official Houdini Séances, the attempt to contact Harry Houdini was declared a failure.

Here I was, seven years later, exploring the old opera house in search of ghosts. Visitors entering the Victorian building are greeted by a magnificent red-carpeted twin staircase that sweeps the theatregoers into the Victorian era. Since rehearsals were going on, the crew's access was restricted to the main floor, which houses the bar, ticket office, and rest rooms. When I saw the flash of a spirit orb over an antique couch opposite the ladies room, I caught this orb on film. However, evidential as the snapshot is, it cannot convey the strong spiritual essence that pervades the theatre. Only a visit to the Goodspeed Opera House can do the place justice.

It is interesting to note that not far from East Haddam is the town of Moodus, Connecticut. "Moodus" literally means "place of bad noises." According to American Indian lore the source of these sounds is the god Hobomoko, who causes rumbling in the earth below. The "bad noises" and earth tremors center around Mount Tom. In 1760, Dr. Steele settled Mount Tom and he attributed the noises to a "great carbuncle" blocking the cave. In time, Dr. Steele and the carbuncle disappeared; however, the noises did not. Some citizens of Moodus say they are caused by earth tremors, while others still believe they return when Hobomoko is displeased.[1]

Gillette Castle, East Haddam, Connecticut. *Photographer : Elaine Kuzmeskus*

Opposite Page:
Goodspeed Opera
House, East Haddam,
Connecticut. *Photogra-
pher: Elaine Kuzmeskus*

Directions

Gillette Castle
67 River Road
East Haddam, CT
Telephone: (860) 526-2331
From Hartford: Take 91 South to Route 9 South to Exit 7 and go
left on 82 East. Then take a right onto River Road.

Goodspeed Opera House
6 Main Street
East Haddam, CT
Box Office: (860) 873-8668.
From Hartford: Go south on I-91 to Exit 22S (left-hand exit).
South on Route 9 to Exit 7. Turn left at the end of the ramp
(ramp is three miles long). At first stoplight, turn right. Theatre is
on right-hand side, just over the bridge.

Chapter Eight

New Haven Hauntings

New Haven was once one of the Connecticut colony's busiest seaports, and also the site of phantom ships that never made their destinations. The first of the phantom ships, the *Fellowship*, was chartered by George Lamberton, a New Haven merchant in 1645/6. The ship, built in Rhode Island, was laded with peas, wheat, hides form the West Indies, and beaver pelts. The voyage, scheduled for the fall, was ill fated from the start. It was delayed until December when the crew had to chop through ice for three miles in order to get to open sea. The ship and it seventy member crew were never heard from again. In the spring, people saw a cloud in the shape of the *Fellowship*, which many believed to be a phantom ship. Longfellow, intrigued by the supernatural event, wrote a poem about *The Phantom Ship*.

New Haven is also synonymous with Yale University. Founded in 1701 in the home of Abraham Pierson, its first rector, in Killingworth. The school moved to New Haven in 1716. Later the school was named Yale College after its benefactor, Elihu Yale, who donated nine bales of goods, 417 books, and a portrait and the arms of King George I. This venerable institution has educated United States Presidents and leaders throughout the world.

It is also home to the Skull and Bones Club — a secret society that included President George W. Bush (Yale '68), his father former President George Bush (Yale '48), and grandfather Prescott ('17). The Skull and Bones Club is housed in a windowless Greco-Egyptian building with padlocked iron doors on High Street in the middle of Yale University. Yale's most famous secret society was started by senior William Russell in December of 1832. He and a group of other students decided to form the Eulogian Club, dedicated to Eulogia, the goddess of eloquence. The Yale society took the skull and crossbones as their symbol. It is also rumored that the club boasts a skull claimed to be that of Geronimo.

Geronimo's skull is not the only spooky thing at Yale. Several ghosts are said to haunt the premises. The ghosts, like the Skull and Bones Society, are well-kept secrets. However, one veteran ghost hunter, Hans Holzer, managed to obtain information on the haunted organ in Yale's Woolsley Hall. The organ, fifth largest in the world, is admired by many visitors, including one from the other side. Built in 1903, the noble organ is known for both its size and range. However, the organ was not lucky for two university organists, according to Hans Holzer, as both were forced into premature retirement — Professor Harry Jepson in 1941 and later Frank Bozyan in the 1970s. Professor Jepson, who passed over in 1952, never played the organ again, even though he lived within walking distance of Woolsey Hall. When Frank Borzan retired, he did so reluctantly, confiding in another Yale employee that he felt he was making a great mistake. Within six months, he was dead.[1]

Since then several people have reported strange and melancholy sensations when working with the organ. According to Hans Holzer, one gentleman who worked on the organ was so sure someone was looking over his shoulder that he had to repeatedly look behind him to be sure he was alone! Overwhelmed by the eerie feeling, he refused to work on the organ alone. The curator's wife also felt a presence in the building at the entrance to the basement door.[2] Could it be that the disgruntled spirit of a former organist is trying to keep strangers out?

Other reports of ghosts at Yale center around the library where researchers have seen orbs and ghostly mists. Curious about this, I contacted Mary Dillman, an archivist working on the Seth collection at Yale. When Roberts died, her editor, a Yale graduate, arranged to place her archives in Yale's Sterling Memorial Library as a part of Americana. The library, built in 1930, is a memorial to John William Sterling. Its designer, James Gamble Rogers, remarked the library is "as near to modern Gothic as we dared to make it." While I did not see any ghosts in its Gothic halls, I did encounter some fascinating ESP material as I read the archives of Jane Roberts.

Professors at Yale may view Jane Roberts (1929-1984) as an interesting part of American history of the 1970s; however, parapsychologists the world over regard Roberts as a genuine channeler. Jane Roberts discovered her own channeling ability while she was writing a book on ESP in 1963. "It was as if someone had slipped me an LSD cube on the sly," said Roberts. She devoted the rest of her life, until her death in 1984, to channeling Seth. In her Tuesday evening classes in Elmira, New York, during the late 1960s and 1970s, Seth taught students how to tune into their inner senses with a great deal of good humor.

He also dispensed advice on a broad range of topics from dreams, astral travel, death, parallel universes, and probable selves. Seth's deep philosophical teachings channeled in Roberts living room were eventually fashioned into a book, *The Nature of Personal Reality,* which was required reading for the Seth circle.

As I perused the files on Roberts's early ESP classes, I realized that Seth was an excellent teacher – drawing students in with personal readings. Next, he introduced them to philosophical concepts of altered states of reality and reincarnation. Finally, once he had gotten their full attention, Seth introduced more advanced types of concepts of a multidimensional universe and parallel realities.

Throughout the sessions, he wasn't above some psychic eavesdropping. For example, he would bring up conversations that the students had during their break. Once, he ended a session by saying, "I don't want to be responsible for keeping some husband waiting for his wife," obviously tuning into an irritated husband's thoughts.

The channeled sessions were conducted from 1968 and were held on a regular basis until 1976, eight years before Roberts's death. They reflect the humor and the politics of the sixties and seventies. For example, an indignant Seth says humorously to an ESP student, "I am not a Volkswagen!" While few college students today drive Volkswagens, in the late sixties they were the cars of choice for many students and hippies, as they were relatively inexpensive. Another example of the Seth's gentle humor came when he encouraged a student (also a writer) to be more patient in her marriage, noting that, "Love is noisy. "

To her husband, a Viet Nam protester, Seth explained why so many young men and woman opposed the war. According to Seth, many protesters had given their lives during World War II and were disappointed that their sacrifices for humanity were unappreciated. Their parents chose instead to focus on material consumption, while ignoring basic human rights. No wonder there was such a generation gap.

The body of the Seth sessions encourages ESP students to look within to discover the multidimensional beings they are. Each one, according to Seth, is capable of so much more than they ever realized. As Seth explains, "The soul can be considered as an electromagnetic, energy field, of which you are a part ... a power house of probabilities or probable action, seeking to be expressed ... Your reality existing a particular area of activity in which aggressive equalities thrusting-outward characteristics are supremely necessary to prevent a falling back into infinite possibilities from which you have only lately emerged."[3] Seth, more

than any modern embodied philosopher or psychologists, empha-
sized light and truth — Yale's mottos — "Lux et Veritas."

Perhaps Seth would have had an explanation for this strange
tale of the supernatural that appeared in the *New Haven Union*
late in December 1875. According to ghost researcher, Joseph
Citro, "Mr. X" was given the address of a "convincing" spirit
medium. When Mr. X entered the New Haven home of the medium, he was taken aback, as the room contained only a stove and
a pine box, which the medium used as a spirit cabinet. Soon the
medium set to work. The newspaper reported Mr. X heard "a
tempest of knocks from all parts of the room."[3]

What followed next was truly out of this world. "A dried-up
figure of a little old man dressed in the fashion of a hundred
years ago," reported the *New Haven Union*. He philosophized at
length on cosmic matters. When the old man finished, he offered
to materialize his daughter. A woman's voice was heard to protest, "I don't want to be materialized," amid a whirl of supernatural activity and mayhem.

The frightened reporter and his friend tried to flee, but instead "they were seized by invisible hands and immediately lost
consciousness." When Mr. X became conscious, he was in his
bedroom. He looked up to see the spirit of the old man and his
daughter in the room. According to Mr. X's account, the spirit of
the old man took $700 from Mr. X's safe and informed him that
his friend would remain in the spirit world a few more days.
When the friend did materialize a few days later in New Haven,
he had no memory of the past few days.[4]

Was the story the product of an over-active imagination perhaps brought on by the newly formed Spiritualist movement
sweeping the country? Or was it true? As for the time travel, only
Einstein would know for sure! However, Mr. X is not the only
soul to claim to see spirits materialize in a cabinet. In fact, cabinet mediumship was popular in the late 1800s. The most famous

of the cabinet mediums were the Eddy brothers of Vermont, who were reported to materialize a variety of spirits for amazed sitters, who included Helena Balvatsky and Colonel Olcutt, founders of the Theosophical Society.

What would the learned professors of psychology at Yale think of such stories? Perhaps the day will come when one of its faculty will take such reports seriously and give them the thorough research they deserve. Meanwhile, the ghosts of Yale's past seem to want to shake academia up a bit!

Yale's motto: Lux et Veritas. *Photographer: Elaine Kuzmeskus*

Gothic front doors of Sterling Library, New Haven, Connecticut. *Photographer: Elaine Kuzmeskus*

Jane Roberts. *Photographer: Richard Conz; Courtesy of Robert Butts.*

Directions

Sterling Memorial Library
120 High Street, P.O. Box 208240
Yale University
New Haven, CT 06520
Directions from Hartford: Take Interstate 91 South to Route 15
(Wilbur Cross/Merritt Parkways). From north: Take Exit 61.
Drive south on Whitney Avenue for approximately five miles.
Shortly after the intersection with Sachem Street, the road will
split. Stay to the right. You are now on Temple Street. Take an
immediate right on Trumbull Street, and the next right onto Hill
House Avenue.

Chapter Nine

New London's Ghosts

New London is steeped in history. Just ask Marilyn Davis of the New London Historical Society. To begin with, there is the old cemetery and the Monte Cristo Cottage, the summer home of writer Eugene O'Neil. "Unfortunately — Monte Cristo Cottage is closed for repairs," Marilyn answered when asked about a tour inside. She did her best, though, to show us the sights of New London, pointing out Ledge Lighthouse, just off shore and later the Lighthouse Inn. Both sites are well-documented ghostly hot spots. When Marilyn concluded the guided tour of New London, she casually mentioned, "The Shaw Mansion is open for tours today."

The Shaw Mansion, which also houses the New London Historical Society, turned out to be a good tip. The mansion was built by Nathaniel Shaw, a wealthy colonial ship owner and was once the fanciest house in town. Constructed on what was once the edge of the Thames River, the property had a panoramic view of ships in the New London Harbor. Surrounded by manicured lawns and well-ordered gardens filled with geraniums, snapdragons, purple cornflowers, and a variety of herbs, with a 1780 Gazebo at its center, the lovely grounds must have been a welcome retreat for the prosperous sea merchant.

When dignitaries came to town, they frequently stayed at the Shaw Mansion. In fact, George Washington not only slept there once but twice — first as a commanding officer in the British

Army and later as the commanding general of the Revolutionary War. While the bed Washington slept in is no longer in the Shaw residence, the table he dined on still sits in the mansion. During the Revolutionary War, the Shaw House was used as Connecticut's Naval Office. It is quite fitting that the home of the civic-minded Shaws should now house the New London Historical Society.

In addition to its proud heritage, the mansion is a portal to the past. I found this out quite by accident when I snapped two pictures of the mansion to finish a roll of film filled with other New London landmarks. Both pictures show evidence of paranormal activity. They were taken with a "throw-away" camera and shot without a flash (no flash bulbs are permitted). The photos were taken on the wide landing where the Shaws gathered as a family. The pictures are filled with orbs of varying heights. As can be seen in those pictures, the Shaw clan still gathers in the upstairs landing adjacent to their former bedrooms!

Other New London ghost spots have well-documented by investigators, including the Ledge Light House, Light House Inn, and Monte Cristo Cottage. Of the three, the Ledge Light House (page 95) is the best known, for a ghost dubbed Ernie. The ninety-year-old lighthouse was manned by a lonely lighthouse keeper who committed suicide in the lighthouse after his wife ran off with another man. Sightings have been reported of a sad-faced bearded man in a slicker. Even after a December 1981 séance was held to free "Ernie's spirit," ghostly hands are said to rattle cups and slam doors.[1] A mecca for ghost hunters, hundreds visit the lighthouse each year in search of Ernie.

Less well-known but just as spooky is the nearby Lighthouse Inn. Built in 1902 as the summer home of steel magnate Charles S. Guthrie, the mansion hosted many a gala. Bette Davis and Joan Crawford retreated to the elegant surroundings of the inn in their heyday. Recognized as one of the Prestigious Historic Hotels of America, the Lighthouse Inn continues to attract visitors from all over the country as well as the other side.

In October of 2004, The Atlantic Paranormal Society, better known as TAPS, visited the Lighthouse Inn to investigate the spirit of a bride who is said to have fallen down the stairs at the Inn on her wedding day in 1930. The TAPS investigators presented their findings on the program "Ghost Hunters." While staff at the Inn did report some paranormal activity, no concrete evidence was recovered from the TAPS investigation. However, some unexplained activity was noted, such as a significant drop in temperature, which registered on the researcher's meter. Could it be a ghost or ghosts were present? Possibly, for a chill on the back of the neck is frequently noted by mediums to be a sign that a spirit is present. Also, Steve, one of the investigators, reported that he did feel someone touch him on the back while he was alone in the inn. However, no orbs or mists were seen on camera. Could it be the ghostly bride is camera shy?

New London is also home to Monte Cristo Cottage, once the summer home of Nobel-Prize winning author Eugene O'Neil. Now it is a museum. O'Neil's finest play, *A Long Day's Journey Into Night,* was fashioned from his memories of childhood summers in New London. In the play, the family dynamics are similar to those of the O'Neils, known for family addictions. Eugene O'Neil, along with his father and brother, waged a life-long battle with alcoholism, while his mother, like the mother in the play, was addicted to morphine.

Standing on the porch of the spacious cottage (page 97) facing the ocean, one can readily envision O'Neil's mother seated in a white wicker chair waiting for the young Eugene and his brother to return from a day at the beach, just a block away. Perhaps some of the early days spent at Monte Cristo Cottage were playful ones for Ella Quinlan O'Neil. However, the family certainly had its troubles. Mrs. O'Neil, for example, trapped in an unhappy marriage, turned to morphine for relief. She spent many a brooding day alone in her upstairs bedroom of Monte Cristo. Once, when unable to get a fix, she even attempted suicide. No wonder visitors report hearing the sound of her nervous pacing from the upstairs bedroom and feel a sudden drop in temperature.

New London County has not only been home to writers such as Eugene O'Neil, but many artists as well. Old Lyme, a few miles south of the City of New London, for example, is known for its artist's colony. In the summer of 1899, artist Henry Ward Ranger rented a room from Florence Griswold. Griswold, the daughter of a wealthy sea captain, had fallen on hard financial times, so she opened her elegant 1882 Greek Revival home to boarders. Soon other artists followed. When Childe Hassam arrived in 1903, so did impressionism. It wasn't long before Old Lyme became an artist's colony.

Perhaps nowhere is the spirit of the colony more present than in the home of its patron, Florence Griswold, which is now a museum (page 96). Miss Florence's love of beauty is everywhere from the sumptuous gardens to rooms filled with antiques to the second floor gallery which houses with the works of the artists she adored. Two spots in particular seem to have a strong presence — the dining room, which is decorated with panels artists painted in appreciation of their stay, and the side porch where Willard Metcalf, Matilda Browne, Frank Dumond, William Chadwick, and Childe Hassam were known to gather. Also, the gardens seem to evoke Miss Florence's spirit. While no pictures were permitted inside the house, the crew took pictures of the gardens and side porch. We didn't get any orbs, but the presence of spirit is definitely there. Miss Florence seemed to be directing me though the gardens down to the river bank, a favorite spot for artists to paint.

When this remarkable woman died in 1937, *The New York Times* noted her passing with this tribute: "This generous spirit survives; not in the Griswold house alone, but as part of an inconsiderable chapter in the history of native art."

Ledge Light House, New London, Connecticut. *Photographer: Marianne Alibozak*

Florence Griswold House, Lyme, Connecticut. *Photographer: Marianne Alibozak*

Side Porch of the Florence Griswold House where the artists would gather after dinner. *Photographer: Elaine Kuzmeskus*

Monte Cristo Cottage, New London, Connecticut. *Photographer: Marianne Alibozak*

Directions

Florence Griswold Museum
96 Lyme Street
Old Lyme, CT 06371
Telephone: (860) 434-5542
From Hartford: Take I-91 South to Route 9 South. Follow Route
9 to the end and get on I-95 going North and follow the directions above. Take EXIT 70; at the bottom of the exit ramp, turn
LEFT at light onto Route 156. Turn RIGHT at second traffic
light onto Halls Road. Take Halls Road to the end. At the end,
take a LEFT at the light onto Lyme Street.

Ledge Lighthouse
Telephone: (860) 442-2222
From Hartford: Take Interstate 95 South to New London. The
sixty-five foot high lighthouse can be seen in New London Harbor.

Lighthouse Inn
6 Gunthrie Place
New London, CT 06320
Telephone: (860) 443-8411
From Hartford: Take 91 South to I-95 South, take Exit 84 S and
keep left at the fork in the ramp to CT-32 (which becomes Eugene O'Neill Dr.) Follow Eugene O'Neill Dr. to the end. At the
intersection go left, then right at the next light onto Bank Street.
At the first light (on Bank St.) go left on Howard St. Stay on
Howard — at the first traffic circle take the third exit, which will
take you to the second traffic circle. At the second traffic circle,
take the first exit — (Pfizer Offices will be on your left) this road
is Pequot Ave. Take Pequot Ave. about 1.5 miles to Guthrie Place
— the Inn is at the end of the street.

Monte Christo Cottage
325 Pequot Avenue
New London, CT 06320
Telephone: (860) 443-0051.
From Hartford: Take Interstate 95 South to New London. The
cottage museum is located on Pequot Avenue between Plant and
Thames streets.

Chapter Ten

The Devil in Tolland

The devil uses many tools: false accusations, greed, and pestilence. All three elements were present at the Daniel Benton Homestead in Tolland. The property was originally purchased by Nathaniel and Rebecca Goldsmith in the 1600s, during a particularly bleak period in Connecticut's history when many of its citizens were falsely accused of the crime of witchcraft.

Such was the case with the Greensmiths. When one of their neighbors, Ann Cole, fell ill with "diabolical possession," she accused Nathaniel and Rebecca Greensmith and another neighbor, Elizabeth Seager, of consorting with the devil, thus causing her illness. When both Greensmiths were put to the water test, in which the their right thumb was tied to the left toe and left thumb to the right toe, they somehow managed to stay afloat! Their survival only further incited the townspeople as they used the feat as evidence the Greeensmiths had made a pact with the devil, otherwise they would have drowned. Nathaniel was stuck to his story of innocence, but the sensitive Rebecca broke down and admitted her guilt, claiming lewd acts, chief among which was admission that "the devil had frequent carnal knowledge of her body." She was found guilty and executed.

In a strange twist of fate, Ann Cole later benefited from the death of the Greensmiths when she married Andrew Benton, a widower who bought the property the couple was forced to give up. In 1720, he built a center chimney colonial home with four fireplaces. Given the value of the Greensmith property, could jealousy or greed have been the motive? Certainly, the Greensmiths were given little opportunity, save the water test, to defend themselves.

In any event, the Benton home was not a healthy one. Several relatives later died of small pox there. One, a fiancé of a woman named Jemima, died during the Civil War era. Jemima, who cared selflessly for her fiancé, also contracted smallpox and later died a lonely death. Visitors to the Benton House have reported seeing an apparition of a woman dressed in the fashion of the 1800s silently walking around the property. Other people report hearing men's voices in the basement. Some even report feeling a terrible sadness as well. Could it be Jemima is still grieving for her lost love? Or is it a lament from Nathaniel and Rebecca Greensmith who were judged to be in consort with the devil?

The Benton home, which remained in family hands until 1932, is now owned and maintained by the Tolland Historical Society. When I visited the Benton property on a July afternoon, while it was hot as Hades, the devil was not on my mind. However orbs, mist, and other evidence of spirits captured on film were.

Were any spirits still present at the Benton Homestead? "Yes." I definitely felt a male presence near the house. Sure enough, the spirit orb appeared just above Ron's shoulder as an orb seen in the picture on page 104. I sensed a benevolent spirit of a gentleman just watching out like he might well have done two hundred years ago.

There have been other strange happenings recorded in other parts of Tolland County as well. For example, in August 1982 John Fuller and David Buckley, two dairy farm workers, spotted a seven-foot humanoid creature when they walked into a dairy barn in Ellington. They described the creature as about 300 pounds with the head of a human, but the nose of an animal. The creature fled, leaving one to wonder what it was. Could it be

Connecticut's version of Big Foot; or perhaps the devil, who can take many forms, was out to scare two innocent country boys? In any event, the report was taken seriously by Sergeant Fred Bird of the Connecticut State Police who was called in to investigate. Discounting the possibility of a practical joke, Sergeant Bird quipped: "You play a practical joke like that around a farm and you are likely to end up dead."[1]

Not too far from the Ellington dairy farm is Caprilands Herb Farm in Coventry. Caprilands was established in 1929 by Adelma Simmons, who lived in a rustic eighteenth century farmhouse surrounded by thirty acres. Her love of gardening and research on herbs were responsible for the phenomenal success of Caprilands. A prolific writer, Adelma Simmons wrote dozens of books on the history, culinary, and medicinal aspects of herbs. Her book, *Gardening in Five Seasons,* has been used as a handbook by countless gardeners. Today, at Caprilands there are over thirty herb gardens such as the Shakespeare Garden, which was one of Mrs. Simmons's favorites.

I met Adelma Simmons in 1974 as a newcomer to Connecticut. Caprilands was the place to go for young people interested in herbs. Herbs were on the menu in the form of cold strawberry soup and rosemary chicken with rice served that June afternoon. When I met Mrs. Simmons, then in her seventies, she sat in her dining room with a pile of books behind her as her patiently answered questions on her favorite topic. "Have you ever researched the astrologer and herbalist William Lily?" I enquired. "Yes," she answered. "In fact, I have a copy of one of his books I picked up in London." I also enquired about the statues of Saint Fiacre, the patron saint of gardeners, and the many statues of Saint Francis that peppered the property. Mrs. Simmons smiled, "Saint Francis in my favorite saint." With the last tidbit, she captured the hearts of many in the room.

While Adelma Simmons passed away in December of 1997, her charismatic spirit is still evident at Caprilands, which looks pretty much as it did thirty years ago. As I casually strolled around the herb gardens, I was drawn one of the sundials — a symbol of eternal life. "Yes," I thought, " she is here." I also felt her presence very strongly in the old shop, which dispensed her many books on herbs and gardening. I could also see her wise face peering out behind the cash register. While the camera did register one orb, in the barn, the real spirit present was that of Adelma Simmons, who single-handedly created a special piece of herb heaven on earth.

After sightseeing in Coventy, take a ride down the road to Nathan Hale Homestead. Visitors can't help but tune into the patriotic spirit of Revolutionary War hero, Nathan Hale. Born on this site in 1755, Hale graduated from Yale University at eighteen. The studious young man began his career as a schoolmaster in East Haddam and later New London, Connecticut. If it were not for the Revolutionary War, Nathan Hale would have lived the quiet life of a scholar.

In July of 1775, the patriotic school teacher volunteered to fight for his ideals. When British troops invaded the New York area, Captain Hale and his men drove the redcoats out. On another occasion, Hale and his man captured a British supply ship. When George Washington needed information on the position of British troops, Hale volunteered for the dangerous spy assignment. Disguised as a Dutch schoolmaster, Hale was able to infiltrate the British lines and obtain vital information on their military strength and positions. Just as he was about to return to the American side, Nathan Hale was captured by the British at Huntington Beach, Long Island, on September 21, 1776. Many believe his cousin, a British loyalist, may have betrayed Hale. In any event, the British commander, General William Howe, sentenced Nathan Hale to death for acts of espionage.

Before he was executed, Hale was reported to uttered these famous words, "I regret that I have only one life to give to my country."

After Hale's death, his father, Deacon Richard Hale, expanded the homestead to accommodate his growing family of twelve children and those of a widow he had recently wed. The home was rebuilt into a two-family house. Unfortunately the homestead where Hale was born later fell into disrepair. In 1914, a New Haven patent attorney purchased the neglected home in order to honor Hale's historic sacrifice for his country. Since then the Hale family home has become a museum and major tourist attraction in Tolland County.

The day I visited, a wedding was taking place on the grounds, so the home was not open to the public. That did not stop me from taking a stroll around the elegant grounds that surround the Georgian house. As I peered in the distance, I could clairvoyantly see shadowy figures of men in Revolutionary War uniforms still marching with muskets. Apparently, the spirits of the great men who sacrificed their lives for our present freedom still like to muster.

Opposite page:
One of the many statues of Saint
Francis that pepper Caprilands,
Coventry, Connecticut Gardens.
Photographer: Elaine Kuzmeskus

Thomas Benton Homestead. *Photgrapher: Elaine Kuzmeskus*

Directions

Daniel Benton Homestead.
Metcalf Road
Tolland, CT 06089
Telephone: (860) 974-1875
From Hartford: Take 84 west to Exit 68. Follow Grant Hill Road
to Metcalf Road.

Caprilands
534 Silver Street
Coventry, CT 06038
Telephone: (869) 742-7244
From Hartford: Take I 84 to Coventry Exit 67. Then follow Route
31 south. Turn left at the junction of Silver Street. Once past the
open fields on Silver Street, you will see Caprilands Herb Farm
on the right.

Nathan Hale Homestead
229 South Street
Coventry, CT 06238
From Hartford: Take I 84 to Coventry Exit 67. Then follow Route
31 south. Turn left at the junction of Silver Street. At the end of
Silver Street turn onto South Street and continue to the homestead.

Chapter Eleven

Windham County: The Unquiet Northeast Corner of Connecticut

Many consider Windham County to be the quiet corner of Connecticut. However, few would consider Willimantic on the south side of the county to be a sleepy town. Visitors to Willimantic are greeted by statues of giant frogs sitting on spools of thread on the entrance to the town bridge. The statues represent the thriving thread industry of the 1800s and the frogs, an incident that occurred when the town was first settled.

Sadly the mills have long since shut down, leaving the fanciful frogs as a reminder of better days. Willimantic in now known as "heroin town," an image residents are trying to overcome. Like any town in decline, Willimantic has its share of saints and sinners. Nowhere is the dichotomy more obvious than in the inhabitants of two of its more historic structures: the Hooker Hotel and the First Spiritualist Church of Willimantic.

The Hooker Hotel, named after General Hooker, was once a pleasant stop for many a traveler from Boston or New York. However, not all of the former residents seem to have checked out. "There's spirits in some of the rooms. I've seen them. So have others," says Wendi Clark, a recovering heroin addict who lived in the hotel from 1996 to 1999. "Some of the rooms have seen a lot of overdoses. I once saw the face of a man reflected in the door of my microwave. Some of the communal bathrooms — you go in and you feel someone else is there, even though you're alone. It's creepy."[1]

The old Windham Hotel also has unregistered visitors. As the story goes, a woman many in town considered a witch was killed there. Her ghost has been heard by many guests late at night. Some also report the unsettling sounds of a baby crying when there are no babies on the premises. Could it be the hotel is haunted?

While disturbed souls — living and dead — have been reported at the Hooker and old Windham hotels, more saintly spirits congregate over at the Willimantic Spiritualist Church. Located at 268 High Street, the old building looks like it has seen better days. However, once inside, the atmosphere becomes dense with the presence of spirits. Thousands of messages from spirits have been delivered from the podium by the many mediums who have served the church, such as the late Rev. Carl Hewitt.

Reverend Hewitt trained at the Willimantic Spiritualist Church back in the early 1970s. At the time Hewitt was the owner of a prosperous hair salon in Gales Ferry, Connecticut, and becoming a medium was the farthest thing from his mind. Born with the gift of clairvoyance, he had long learned to suppress his gift. Growing up in the South in the 1940s and '50s, clairvoyance was the gift of the devil!

However, Hewitt's spirit guides had other plans for him. As Carl Hewitt explains, one morning he received an unusual phone call, "You are to go to Willimantic to a class dealing with psychic phenomena at seven o'clock tonight." The forty-one-year-old beauty salon owner couldn't make head or tails of the call, so he decided to ignore it. There was no way he could go anyway as Thursday was his busiest night. Later, when four customers canceled their appointments, he decide to go out of curiosity.

Not even sure of the direction, Carl Hewitt got in his car and headed for Willimantic. It wasn't long before he heard another strange voice that directed him to Valley Street, then to the church. When he entered the church, a circle was already in session and the medium, an elderly man who had his back to Carl Hewitt, said: "You're Carl Hewitt, I've been expecting you."[2]

No sooner did he join the circle than Hewitt fell asleep. When he woke up, he apologized to the group. Everyone laughed. Apparently Carl Hewitt was not asleep but in a trance — an aspect of mediumship in which a spirit speaks through the sleeping medium. Most people sit in a weekly circle for several years before even developing basic mediumship. Few reach the level of trance of an Edgar Cayce or Andrew Jackson Davis. After his dramatic entrance into Spiritualism, Carl Hewitt became a regular member of the Thursday night circle and later was ordained as a minister of the National Spiritual Alliance of Churches, June 2, 1974.

Rev. Carl Hewitt went to become one of Connecticut's most successful mediums, maintaining an office in Colchester, Connecticut. In 1980, my husband Ron took classes with Carl Hewitt. In the first session, which was the only class we attended together, Ron had a most amazing experience. After we formed a circle of about eighteen woman and four men, Rev. Hewitt turned off the lights and played a relaxing tape filled with the sounds of nature.

The tape worked beautifully. Within minutes, I dropped from the waking state to a deep level of relaxation. However, when the lights went on I was deeply disturbed at the sight of my husband seated on the other side of the room, his normal ruddy complexion was stark white and he had a frightened look in his blue eyes. "What's the matter?" I whispered. "I'll tell you later," Ron replied as Rev. Hewitt began his lecture on the gifts of the spirit.

While driving back to Suffield, Ron related the most unusual experience. Once the meditation music had begun, he immediately left his body and remained out of body for the entire meditation. "Elaine," he said with conviction, "I could not get back in

— the whole time I was on the ceiling." When the thirty-minute meditation tape ended, my husband did return to his body, which remained sleeping on the chair below during our meditation. "Ron, that is great," I reassured him. "People meditate for years to reach that state of out-of-body awareness."

If you are interested in learning more about meditation, mediumship or out-of-body experiences, there are many Spiritualist churches throughout Connecticut, listed at the end of the chapter. A good way to get to know a church is to attend a Sunday service. If the vibrations seem right, you may wish to join a weekly development circle as well.

Pine Grove Spiritualist Camp. Norwich, Connecticut. *Photographer: Marianne Alibozak*

Directions

Hooker Hotel
877 Main Street
Willimantic, CT
Telephone: (860) 423-7150)
From Hartford: Take 91 South to I-291. Merge onto I 384 East, which will become 6 East. Follow 6 East onto ramp CT-I95/ University of Connecticut. Take the ramp toward Willimantic business district. 6 East becomes Route 66 or Main Street. Proceed to 817 Main Street.

Willimantic Spiritualist Church, Willimantic, Connecticut
268 High Street
Willimantic, CT 06226-1340
(860) 423-5774
From Hartford: Take 91 South to 1-291. Merge onto I 384 East, which will become 6 East. Follow 6 East onto ramp CT-I95/ University of Connecticut. Take the ramp toward Willimantic business district. Turn right onto High Street and proceed to 268, which is on the right.

Connecticut Spiritualist Churches

New London Spiritualist Church
2 Moore Court
New London, CT 06320-4918
Telephone: (860) 440-3150

The Church of the Infinite Spirit
Masonic Temple
80 Walsh Avenue
Newington, CT 06111-2847
Telephone: (860) 582-7385

National Spiritualist Church of Norwich, Inc.
29 Park Street (Off Main Street)
Norwich, CT 06360
Telephone: (860) 886-8522

Albertson Memorial Church
293 Sound Beach Avenue Box 143
Old Greenwich, CT 06870-0143
(Telephone: 203) 637-4615

First Spiritualist Church of Willimantic
268 High Street
Willimantic, CT 06226-1340
Telephone: (860) 423-5774

Pine Grove Spiritualist Camp
34 South Pine Street
Niantic, CT 06357
Telephone: (860) 739-2157

Chapter Twelve

"Cleansing Negative Ghosts"

When Lord Carnarvon opened King Tutankhamen's tomb in 1923, he neglected to read the hieroglyphics inscribed on the arched doorway. If he had, he might have had second thoughts, as the ancient Egyptians chiseled: "Death to he who enters this tomb." However, he was too excited. Both he and his archeologist, Howard Carter, had spent years searching for the tomb of Tutankhamen. Two weeks later, April 5 at 2 a.m., Lord Carnarvon died from an infected insect bite at age fifty-three. At that same moment all the light went out over Cairo![1]

Had Lord Carnarvon read *The Egyptian Book of the Dead*, he would have taken the warning very seriously. The ancient Egyptians were masters of curses and could manipulate both white and black magic. The Egyptians, like the ancient Chinese sages, understood that life has both good and evil, positive and negative — what the Chinese term "yin-yang. The yin-yang symbol is half a white circle with a small black dot, and half a black circle with a small white dot to symbolize the balance between dark and light. It reminds the seeker that each saint has some negative and that within each evildoer, there is still a bit of light.

Edgar Cayce, "the Sleeping Prophet," is an example of a man who dedicated his life to the light. He dedicated his life to channeling medical clairvoyant readings from a spiritual presence known as "the Source." However, occasionally other entities would come through Cayce — some very high like the archangel

Gabriel; others, like Halaliel, were not as high. While Cayce's Source stated, "Halaliel is the one who from the beginning has been a leader of the heavenly host, who has defied Ariel, who has made the ways that have been heavy — but has the means for the UNDERSTANDING." Others were not so sure. Recent Cayce experts now question Halaliel's identity. Some believe that Halaliel may have been a negative entity posing as an angel, as much of the information given by Halaliel as not come to pass.

If a wise man such as Cayce could be fooled, how easy it is to dupe the unsuspecting ghost hunter who may be called on to assist those plagued by negative ghosts. That is why it is most important to keep an even mind while ghost hunting. Make sure you are protected by prayer, affirmation, right intention, and the presence of sincere seekers in your party. Any tension or negativity in the group can draw in negative energy and less than positive ghosts. Few citizens of Connecticut are more aware of the battle of good and evil than Ed and Lorraine Warren. The Warrens, nationally known ghost hunters, have written several books on the subject. Lorraine Warren, a natural clairvoyant and light trance medium, has been investigated by Dr. Thelma Moss of UCLA.

The Warrens have been investigating hauntings, apparitions, and demons for over forty years — writing best sellers such as *The Devil in Connecticut,* which chronicles a Brookfield case of possession. In the early 1980s, David Glatzel murdered his friend Arne Johnson after a series of horrifying paranormal events. The Warrens were also called in to investigate the Amityville home of the unfortunate DeFeo family, who were murdered by their oldest son.

One of the most interesting cases of poltergeist activity the Warrens investigated occurred on Lindley Street in Bridgeport. The Goodin family moved into a four-room home with their daughter, Marcia, a sad child whose only friend was her cat, Sam.

When Sam returned from a visit to the veterinarian, he had changed. Marcia's father, Gerald Goodin, claimed, "the cat would kick at the basement door, yelling, 'Let me out, you dirty Frenchman, you dirty Greek!'" The poltergeist activity that followed was even more unsettling — doors banged, dishes rattled, and a heavy leather chair even levitated six inches. According to Bridgeport police records, officers saw the refrigerator rise about six inches off the floor as well as a twenty-one-inch portable television lift off a table and rotate. In November 1974, the Warrens were called in. They pinpointed Marcia as the source of the negativity energy. Apparently, the unhappy girl also dabbled in the occult. While Ed and Lorraine rate the case as "a 10 on a one-to-10 scale" of supernatural things they've seen in their fifty years of experience, others in the community claimed it was a hoax of a disturbed child.[2]

Currently, Ed and Lorraine Warren direct the New England Society of Psychic Research. The Warrens, who are deeply religious, believe it is important that each member of a family be baptized to prevent negative psychic activity such as a haunting. They also suggest tossing out any Ouija™ boards in the house. According to the Warrens, "ninety percent of their worst cases begin with a Ouija board." Also, make sure each room has a religious icon such as a crucifix and picture of Jesus, or Buddha, or Mother Mary. Should a negative spirit be present itself, the Warrens advise, "In your bravest, most commanding voice, shout 'In the name of Jesus Christ (or the appropriate deity for your faith) I command you to leave this place and go back to where you came from!'"

Negative spirits can disrupt the rhythm and harmony of the home if not dealt with swiftly. Psychologist Dr. Edith Fiori and Dr. William Baldwin believe that unwanted spirits can actually possess a person, causing depression, anxiety, and even psychosis. In severe cases, spirit releasement therapy may be used. Dr

William Baldwin and his wife, Dr. Judith Baldwin, specialize in this procedure. Their method utilizes prayer, hypnosis, and clairvoyance to get rid of negative energy.

Many energy workers recommend smudging as a means of clearing the body of negative energy. Start with a prayer of intent: "You are surrounded and protected by Divine energy." Then light a sage or sandalwood incense stick and trace the person's outline with the stick. The smoke acts as a conduit for the positive intent of clearing energy and will gently clear the auric field. You can also use smudging to clear a hotel room, classroom, or even your home after the stale smoke and negative vibes of a party.

A second method is to imagine a shower of white light about three feet above your head. Imagine the white light cascading down your head, covering the whole body. Stay in the energy shower for a few minutes until your aura is cleared.

A third method to clear your aura is to sit under a full moon. This exercise works best if you sit outside, but if it is too cold, sit inside and stare out at the moon. Once seated in a comfortable position, stare at Mother Moon in silence for ten minutes or more. Feel her light surround you, removing any emotional pain or negative thoughts from the astral body. Allow your heart energy to expand. Soon, you will feel like a new woman (or man).

Moon energy can also be used to clear an article. This is especially true of crystals and sacred articles. You can place them under a full moon for twenty-four hours or wash them in sea salt and water. You can even clear the energy of a room by using a concentration of a quarter cup of sea salt to a quart of water, placed in a bottle with an atomizer. Gently mist the walls. Then smudge the room with sage and a prayer of intention: "This room is surrounded and filled with Divine energy."

The Celts used to pour salt around the foundation of their houses to keep bad energy at bay. They also believed in putting a mirror in a window in every room for protection. The mirror, which faces outward, is said to turn away unwanted ghosts. Other cultures swear by burning a white bee's wax candle, using rose or lavender scented oils or burning sandalwood or frankincense and myrrh incense for protection.

Not only do individuals and homes need psychic cleansing but public places as well. I was called on once to exorcise not just a house but a whole theatre when I conducted a séance following the play, *Blythe Spirit,* which was playing at the Long Wharf Theater in the spring of 1998. While the cast was excited about a séance, some members were concerned that the spirits might linger after the séance. "Not a problem," I said. " I can exorcise the theatre after the séance." My assistant, Springfield psychometrist Ceil Lewonchuk, and I had a grand time bringing through loved ones for the audience. Ceil even tuned into the resident ghost as well – "Paddy," an older gentleman who volunteered many hours to the Long Wharf before his death. Then, we smudged the Long Wharf Theater in the wee hours of the morning. Ceil took one side, and I took the other and set to work smudging every inch. It wasn't long before we reached the corners of the theater. We were both surprised at how much negative energy had accumulated there. Apparently negative spirits like dark corners!

From then on I have made it a point to clear the energy, especially when I do out-of-town seminars. In September 2004, I did a workshop for the Learning Exchange in New York City. I arrived two hours early to smudge and clear the room before the students arrived for their "Dreams and Astral Travel" seminar. After the smudging session, I was looking out the window, reflecting on the beauty of the Empire State Building at sunset, and snapped a photo. When I developed the snapshot, I was surprised to see that I was not alone. Multiple orbs appeared in the snapshot to indicate the many positive spirits were wishing to enlighten humanity. In fact, the positive spirits in the world far outweigh the negative ones. The goal of life, after all, is not one of death but immortality.

> From the unreal lead me to the real.
> From darkness lead me onto light
> From death lead me into immortality

— Hindu Prayer

Opposite Page:
Multitude of orbs
appeared in this picture
of the Empire State
Building. *Photographer:
Elaine Kuzmeskus*

Endnotes

Chapter Two

1. Frank Podmore, *Mediums of the Nineteenth Century, Volume II*, University Press, New York, pages 230-231.
2 and 3. Rosemary Guiley, *Harper's Encyclopedia of Mystical and Paranormal Experiences*, Harper Publishers, New York, 428.
4. Samuel Schreiner, *The Passionate Beechers*, John Wiley and Sons, New York, 2003, page 25.
5. Samuel Schreiner, *The Passionate Beechers*, John Wiley and Sons, New York, 2003, page 253.
6. Samuel Schreiner, *The Passionate Beechers*, John Wiley and Sons, New York, 2003, page 256.
7. Samuel Schreiner, *The Passionate Beechers*, John Wiley and Sons, New York, 2003, page 332.
8. Ruth Brandon, *The Spiritualists*, Alfred Knopf, New York, 1983, pages 206-7.
9 http//www.emory.edu/Education/ William James Biography,/Chronology/ and Photographs, page 17.

Chapter Four

1. Samuel Schreiner, *The Passionate Beechers*, John Wiley and Sons, New York, 2003, page 235.
2. Sandra L. Katz, *Dearest of Geniuses*, 2003, Tide-Mark Press, Windsor, CT, page 76.
3. Sandra L. Katz, *Dearest of Geniuses*, 2003, Tide-Mark Press, Windsor, CT, page 116.
4. Sandra L. Katz, *Dearest of Geniuses*, 2003, Tide-Mark Press, Windsor, CT, page 3.

Chapter Five

1. Troy Taylor, Internet article, "The Stratford Poltergeist," prairie ghosts.com
2. Internet article "The Stratford Poltergeist" by Troy Taylor prairie ghosts.com
3. Cosmic society/ union htm, page 2

Chapter Six

1. Ghost village.com/legends/Dudleytown.htm., page 3

Chapter Seven

1. Hans Holzer, *More Where the Ghosts Are,* Citadel Press, 2002, page 31 and 32.

Chapter Eight

1. Hans Holzer, *Ghosts,* Workman Publishing Company, New York, NY, 1996, page 552.
2. Hans Holzer, *Ghosts,* Workman Publishing Company, New York, NY, 1996, page 553.
3. Jospeh Citro, *Passing Strange,* Hounton Mifflin Company, Boston, MA, page 299.
4. Jospeh Citro, *Passing Strange*, Hounton Mifflin Company, Boston, MA, page 299.

Chapter Nine

1. Dennis William Hauck, *Haunted Places: The National Directory,* Penguin Books, 2002, page 96.
2. Dennis William Hauck, *Haunted Places: The National Directory,* Penguin Books, 2002, page 96.

Chapter Ten

1. Joseph Citro, *Passing Strange*, Houghton Mifflin Co, Boston, MA, 1997, page 193.

Chapter Eleven

1. Tracy Gordon Fox, "Death at Hotel Hooker," *The Hartford Courant,* October 21 2002.
2. Judith Joslow-Rodwald and Patricia West-Barker, *Healing Spirits,* Crossing Press, Berkeley, CA, 2001, page 60.

Chapter Twelve

1. Alan Vaughan, *Incredible Coincidence*, Ballantine Books, New York, page 114-116.
2. New England Society for Psychical Research Warren Web Site, Copyright © 1998 - 2004 by Ed and Lorraine Warren.

Bibliography

Books and Articles

Brandon, Ruth. *The Spiritualists*. New York: Alfred Knopf, 1983.

Cahill, Bob. "Phelps Mansion: History." www.prsne. comphelps_mansion.htm

Citro, Joseph. *Passing Strange*. Boston, Massachusetts: Houghton Mifflin, 1997.

Fox, Tracy Gordon. "Death at Hotel Hooker." *The Hartford Courant*, October 21, 2002.

Gauld, A. *The Founders of Psychical Research*. London: Routledge and Kegan, Paul, 1968.

Grant, Ellsworth S. "Connecticut's Witch Hunt. The Hartford Courant." *Northeast Magazine*, October 28 1984.

Guiley, Rosemary Ellen. *Encyclopedia of Ghosts and Spirits*. New York: Harper Publishers, 1992.

Harris, Gale Jan FASG, "Connecticut Witch: William and Goodwife Ayres of Hartford." *American Genealogist,* July 2000.

Hauck, Dennis William. *Haunted Places: The National Directory.* New York: Penguin Books, 1996.

Hoadly, Charles L.L.D, "The Case Of Witchcraft in Hartford." *Connecticut Magazine*, November 1899.

Holzer, Hans. *Ghosts*. New York: Workman Publishing Company, 1996.

Holzer, Hans. *More Where the Ghosts Are*. New York: Citadel Press, 2002.

Jarman, Rufus. "Mystery House on Elm Street." *Yankee Magazine,* 1971.

Joslow-Rodwald, Judith and Patricia West-Barker. *Healing Spirits.* Berkley, California: Crossing Press, 2001.

Katz, Sandra L. *Dearest of Geniuses.* Windsor, Connecticut: Tide-Mark Press, 2003.

Norman, Michael and Beth Scott. *Haunted America.* New York: Tom Doherty, 1994.

Podmore, Frank. *Mediums of the Nineteenth Century, Volume II.* New York: University Press, 1963.

Schreiner, Samuel. *The Passionate Beechers.* New York: John Wiley and Sons, 2003.

Smith, Susy. *Prominent American Ghosts.* Cleveland, Ohio: World Publishing, 1967.

Taylor, Troy. *Haunting of America.* Decatur, Illinois: Whitechapel Productions, 2001.

Vaughan, Alan. Incredible Coincidence. New York: Ballantine Books,

Vessie, P.R. MD, "Hereditary Chorea: St. Anthony's Dance and Witchcraft in Colonial America." *Journal of the Connecticut State Medical Society.*

Warren, Joshua P. *How to Hunt Ghosts.* New York: Simon & Schuster, 2003.

Internet Sources

Cosmic society/union htm

Ghost village.com/legends/Dudleytown.htm.

http://www.emory.edu/Education/William James Biography,/ Chronology/ and Photograph.

New England Society for Psychical Research Warren Web Site

Taylor, Troy. "The Stratford Poltergeist." prairie ghosts.com

Index